THE WISDOM OF WILDERNESS

ALSO BY GERALD G. MAY

The Dark Night of the Soul

The Awakened Heart

Addiction and Grace

Care of Mind, Care of Spirit

Will and Spirit

Pilgrimage Home

Simply Sane

The Open Way

THE WISDOM

Experiencing the Healing Power of Nature

OF WILDERNESS

GERALD G. MAY

HarperOne

An Imprint of HarperCollinsPublishers

HarperOne

HarperCollins books may be purchased for educational, business, or sales promotional use. For information, please e-mail the Special Markets Department at SPsales@harpercollins.com.

HarperCollins Web site: http://www.harpercollins.com
HarperCollins®, ■■®, and HarperOne™
are trademarks of HarperCollins Publishers.

FIRST HARPERCOLLINS PAPERBACK EDITION PUBLISHED IN 2007

Library of Congress Cataloging-in-Publication Data is available upon request.
ISBN 978–0–06–114663–3

HB 12.22.2017

CONTENTS

ACKNOWLEDGMENTS

The epigraphs preceding each chapter are selected from the beautiful poetry of Saint John of the Cross, a sixteenth-century Spanish Carmelite friar whose writings on the spiritual life have been priceless for me. The quotations come from *The Collected Works of St. John of the Cross*, translated by Kieran Kavanaugh and Otilio Rodriguez © 1979, 1991, by Washington Province of Discalced Carmelites, ICS Publications, 2131 Lincoln Road, N.E., Washington, D.C. 20002, U.S.A. All of the quotations are from the 1991 edition. I am most grateful to the Institute of Carmelite Studies for permission to use this material. For more on John of the Cross, see my book *The Dark Night of the Soul* (San Francisco: HarperSanFrancisco, 2004).

I also wish to thank my advance readers, especially my wife Betty, Jan Thurston, Betsy Moore, Gigi Ross, Gordon Forbes, and June Schulte for her detailed comments and for relaying her son Shiloh's knowledge of bald eagle territorial defense.

FOREWORD

Jerry May knew he was dying as he wrote this book. So he gathered up all the life he could hold with words—as wild creatures gather food against a hard winter—and left us a book so well stocked with love and wisdom, tears and laughter, healing and hope, it can help all of us winter through.

I met Jerry May in the early 1970s in Washington, D.C., where we worked together on several projects. We were young and unformed, but even then I knew I was in the presence of a good man, a brilliant mind, and a great soul. I was a community organizer, university professor, and spiritual neophyte. Jerry was launching out on three decades of profoundly life-giving work with the Shalem Institute, an ecumenical organization and community devoted to reclaiming the Christian contemplative tradition, enriched by insights from Eastern religions.

Signing on with the Shalem Institute was a turning point for this gifted psychiatrist who had served as a medic in Vietnam, a medic who refused to wear a sidearm and later became a conscientious objector. At Shalem, Jerry deepened his birthright gift for contemplation and began to interweave that gift with his psychiatric training. He found a platform for counseling, speaking, and writing from which he supported the spiritual growth of countless grateful people through personal contact and eight widely read, highly regarded books: *The Open Way* (1977), *Simply Sane* (1977), *Pilgrimage Home* (1979), *Will and Spirit* (1987), *Addiction and Grace* (1991), *The Awakened Heart* (1991), *Care of Mind, Care of Spirit* (1992), *The Dark Night of the Soul* (2005). At least two of his books (*Will and Spirit* and *Addiction and Grace*) have attained the status of contemporary classics.

When I met Jerry, he was just beginning to blaze a pioneering trail in the emerging field of contemplative psychology, which is credible and influential today in part because of his work. Without the grounding of psychology, contemplative insight easily becomes untethered, floating above the realities of our embodied lives. Without the transcendence of contemplation, psychology quickly diminishes us, reducing the human mystery to banalities like impulse and impulse management.

Early on, Jerry May became convinced that a contemplative psychology could embrace, in-the-round, the great conundrum of the Word-become-flesh that we call the human self. This, his last book, is rich with evidence that Jerry pursued this conviction until the day he died. In fact, I believe that *The Wisdom of Wilderness* opens new ground in the field Jerry helped to create precisely because of the end-of-life sensibilities he brought to writing it.

In one splendid passage, Jerry writes about his deep-woods encounter with a very large bear who came snuffling around his very thin tent in the middle of a very dark night:

> *I lie unmoving for a very long time after the bear leaves, my senses completely alert, no thoughts, no images, seeing nothing, hearing only my heart and breath and the sounds of the night. For the first time in my life, I am experiencing pure fear. I am completely present in it, in a place beyond all coping because there is nothing to do. I have never before experienced such clean, unadulterated purity of emotion. This fear is naked. It consists, in these slowly passing moments, of my heart pounding, my breath rushing yet fully silent, my body ready for anything, my mind absolutely empty, open, waiting. I am fear. It is beautiful.*

For Jerry, contemplative psychology takes us "beyond all coping" to a place where we need not resist the difficult emotions of life but can become one with them, which helps us become one with ourselves. Looking back on his early psychiatric practice, he criticized himself for spending too much time helping people "cope" with their difficulties:

> *I have come to hate that word, because to cope with something you have to separate yourself from it. You make it your antagonist, your*

enemy. Like management, coping is a taming word, sometimes even a
warfare word. Wild, untamed emotions are full of life-spirit, vibrant
with the energy of being. They don't have to be acted out, but neither do
they need to be tamed. They are part of our inner wilderness; they can
be just what they are. God save me from coping. God help me join, not
separate. Help me be with and in, not apart from. Show me the way to
savoring, not controlling. Dear God, hear my prayer: make me forever
copeless.

Here, in a single vibrant paragraph, are a few of the gifts the reader will find in every chapter of this book: clarity and candor about the author's own journey; psychological insights turned upside down and made more piercing as a result; a turning toward prayer that is more in-your-face than pious; and all of it rendered in clear and compelling prose. What great gifts Jerry May brought to his work! What great gifts he left behind for us to cherish.

Intellectual power and spiritual courage were clearly two of Jerry's gifts; in the words of an ancient theologian, he knew how to think "with the mind descended into the heart." But the impact of his work—the great and lasting legacy of hearts touched and lives transformed that Jerry left behind—would have been impossible, I think, had it not been for a third gift: Jerry possessed a sense of humor rooted in "divine madness." As his family and friends will testify, he always saw the cosmic comedy in the human condition—yours, mine, and his own.

Jerry was fond of quoting lines and sometimes whole sections of sketches from Monty Python's Flying Circus, not the sort of source material acolytes expect their gurus to draw upon! Since guru was a role Jerry disdained for himself, Python served him well. In a meeting he and I attended where the talk had turned to "demon possession," Jerry made the Pythonesque proposal that the best way to exorcise demons was to become such a boring person that the evil spirits would seek a more interesting place to live, a thesis he laid out with an *almost* straight face. And a mutual friend recently told me about a conversation between Jerry and Thich Nhat Hanh, the much-revered Vietnamese Buddhist master, in which Jerry said, "Thich, old buddy, you know how you're always talking about 'this moment, precious moment, only moment.' Well, Thich, some moments really suck." The Pythons would have been proud!

In person, Jerry was a spontaneously funny man who proved Chesterton's famous remark, "The reason angels can fly is that they take themselves so lightly." His unforced humility and utter accessibility allowed people to trust him, face-to-face and on the printed page, with their inner lives. And in his speaking, counseling, and writing Jerry was a teacher who proved William James's insight that "Common sense and a sense of humor are the same thing, moving at different speeds." Using his lightning-fast common sense, Jerry tried to rescue psychiatry and spirituality from their occasional (to put it mildly) pretentiousness, making them, too, trustworthy and accessible to people in need.

Jerry's divine madness was also, I believe, one source of the courage that allowed him to take on tough topics, such as his ground-breaking work on addiction and this book on wilderness.

Wilderness and its terrors is the text here, but courage is the sub-text—the courage to face one's self in the wilderness and the wilderness in one's self. Sometimes you eat the bear and sometimes the bear eats you: how can you face the fearsome bear without seeing the joke?

Dying as he brought *The Wisdom of Wilderness* to completion, Jerry drew on his divine madness as well as his fine mind and strong spirit. "I am sick now," he writes in the preface. "The prospect of my death is continually before me. My body is frail, my energy always at the edge of exhaustion. At the same time, I am wilder than I've ever been before. My soul basks in wilderness, and I am grateful." Imagine: a sick, frail, exhausted, dying man who says he is wilder than ever before, which in Jerry's case is saying something!

There is one more quality at the heart of this good man's life, perhaps the most important of all. Jerry was profoundly in love with his family, his wife Betty and their children Earl, Paul, Greg, Julie, and Chris. When I asked Betty May—Jerry's lifelong love, co-conspirator, and devoted gadfly—about Jerry's relation to his family, she said words I know to be true:

> Nothing—not his searching, not his books, not Shalem—nothing was more important to Jerry than his kids. They were his life and, I believe, his most important legacy. To me, these incredible human beings he left behind define him and explain him more than all his books put together. They reflect his wisdom, his goodness, his laughter, his stubbornness, his intelligence, his wonderings and wanderings, his passion and compassion, his love—everything that was wonderful about Jerry and that still is Jerry today.

Of course, that kind of love cannot be contained within a family. Blessedly, it spills over into a too-often loveless world. Jerry's last words were spoken to his daughter, Julie, but they could have been spoken to any and all of us: "Trust in Love. Trust in God."

With Jerry May's death, we have suffered a great loss. With this book—forged in his living and refined in the crucible of his dying—we have received a great gift. I think Jerry would say that painful but promising paradoxes such as this are at the heart of the wilderness experience, and of the wisdom traditions that have emerged from our encounters with wilderness, both inner and outer. I think Jerry would urge us to go beyond our simpleminded dualism about death and life, to see into—and live into—the wild unity of it all.

Jerry opened his now-classic *Will and Spirit* with these words: "We all have secrets in our hearts. I will tell you one of mine. All my life I have longed to say yes, to give myself completely, to some Ultimate Someone or Something."

I believe that Jerry's longing has been fulfilled. Thanks to this gentle, wild, bright, and beautiful man, our stores of significant thought, authentic prayer, and shake-the-rafters laughter have been replenished, on earth as they now are in heaven.

—*Parker J. Palmer (author of* A Hidden Wholeness,
Let Your Life Speak, The Courage to Teach,
The Active Life, To Know as We Are Known,
and The Company of Strangers)

PREFACE

All who are free tell me a thousand
graceful things of you;
all wound me more, and leave me dying of,
ah, I-don't-know-what.

—SAINT JOHN OF THE CROSS, *SPIRITUAL CANTICLE*

I am sick now. The prospect of my death is continually before me. My body is frail, my energy always at the edge of exhaustion. At the same time, I am wilder than I've ever been before. My soul basks in wilderness, and I am grateful.

Wilderness is not just a place; it is also a state of being. If happiness means being happy and sadness means being sad, then wilderness means being wilder. Look it up, and you'll find that the primary meaning of *wild* is "natural." In turn, *natural* comes from the Latin *nasci,* meaning "to be born." Words like natal, nativity, and native come from the same root, all referring to birth.

Wilderness, then, is not only the nature you find outdoors. It can also refer to your own true Nature—the You that is closest to your birth. This inner wilderness is the untamed truth of who you really are.

The stories that follow are accounts of how, between 1990 and 1995, outdoor Nature acquainted me with my own inner nature: how external wilderness spoke to my internal wilderness, and how it healed me and made me more whole. I was fifty years old in 1990. I had practiced psychiatry for nearly a quarter of a century, and had practiced meditation for almost as long. With all that experience, it might seem odd that I still had so much to learn about my own nature. But I was not so unusual.

In our modern, highly developed culture, nearly all of us are estranged from our true nature, and consequently, from the nature around us. From the time we are little children, we are taught to set ourselves apart from all natural inclinations so that we can control, modify, and restrain them. We have learned to be suspicious, even afraid, of any form of wildness. Some of us are unabashedly destructive of our environment. Others want to protect, manage, and be good stewards of our resources. Still others of us conjure up idealized images of "nature," a pristine paradise when left untouched by human hands. What none of us seems to want, what we all resist, is to admit that we are inevitably, intimately, and irrevocably *part of* Nature rather than *apart from it*.

One of my favorite movie scenes is in John Huston's classic, *The African Queen*. Charlie Allnut (Humphrey Bogart), having had a bit too much to drink the night before, awakens to find Rose

Sayer (Katharine Hepburn) pouring his bottles of gin into the Zambezi River.

"Whatcha bein' so mean for, Miss?" he pleads. "A man takes a drop too much once in a while, it's . . . it's only human nature."

"Nature, Mr. Allnut," she replies, "is what we are put in this world to rise above."

These words express the most fundamental estrangement of Western civilization: the belief that we must dominate and tame all that is wild within and around us. This conviction has wounded us deeply, forever making us feel apart from Nature rather than a part of it. We separate what is natural from what is "man-made." Dams built by beavers are natural, we say, but the dams we build are not. At worst they are an abuse of Nature, at best a management of natural resources.

For the most part, our culture tries to manage inner and outer Nature by force. We separate ourselves from wildness, make it an object at best, an adversary at worst, a thing to be conquered and subjugated. As a result, we have done much damage to the earth and to ourselves. But even when our attitudes shift from domination to caring, even when we desire to heal some of the wounds we have inflicted upon the planet and upon ourselves, we still feel we must be separate and in control. We are always thinking in terms of management: management of natural resources, management of patient care in hospitals, management of our own feelings.

Many cultures—especially those we call primitive—experience no such estrangement. Instead, people of such cultures often reflect a sense of kinship, even union, with the earth and its creatures, and a sense of harmony within themselves. I wonder if we might have been like that too, long ago. If so, what happened to make us feel so separate? Was it our notion of a transcendent God above all creation, who gave us the divine right of dominion over the earth? Or did deeper forces within us shape our insatiable need to improve upon things, our unquenchable thirst for control?

I do not know the cause, but I do know that the fracture between us and nature is still unhealed. It is such an ancient thing that we have become accustomed to the pain of it. And I am convinced that before we can effectively act to heal the wounds we have inflicted upon the earth, we must somehow recover our own natural wholeness. I am further convinced that we cannot do this healing for ourselves; if we could, we would have done so long ago. Only the grace of Something or Someone beyond us can bring us the healing. In my case, the healing came through Nature itself.

For the most part, the stories I tell here are elaborations of my journal entries from those first five years of the 1990s, along with some current reflections and some memories from earlier times. I have arranged them according to themes, so I may tell of something that happened recently, then go back to an account of an earlier time. I hope this will not be confusing; *what* happened in my wilderness experiences is, for me, more important than *when* it happened. I must also acknowledge that some of the accounts are likely to sound like tall tales. It's certainly possible that some of my perceptions were distorted, but I assure you that I have made nothing up. Aside from changing the names of certain places, the stories are as honest and accurate as I can make them.

I am sharing my stories here in the hope that they will encourage ("give heart to") you in your own willingness to be taught and healed by Nature's grace. I'm sure you already have some of your own stories of teaching and healing, and that there will be more to come. By definition, Nature is wild and unpredictable, so your stories won't be the same as mine. My most profound experiences occurred when I was alone outdoors, away from civilization, but it might not be that way for you. You may find your wilderness anywhere: in your own house, your garden, with other people, in the most surprisingly ordinary situations. At this point in my own life I no longer feel called to outdoor solitude. That particular yearning ended in 1995. Now it is the wilderness of my own fragmenting body that offers to heal me—at a level far deeper than physical life. We all need to allow ourselves to be led into our own wildernesses, there to be taught what we most need to know, and to be healed where we most need it.

My stories speak often of a Presence I encountered in the wilderness—or perhaps more accurately One who sought me out and drew me there. I called this Presence "the Power of the Slowing"; it was this Power that seemed to beckon, guide, teach, heal, and show me very deeply who I am. All my life I had longed for such a palpable and immediate encounter with a divine guiding Presence, a feeling of unity with the world. This lifelong prayer was answered during those years in the outdoors, and as I now look back, this may have been Nature's greatest gift to me.

At that time, the Power of the Slowing always seemed to show up in surprising and dramatic ways. For me, it also had a distinctly feminine quality. I identified it with Mother Nature, an ancient female archetype that reaches back to such feminine concepts as Holy Wisdom in the Book of Proverbs, Sophia in Greek philosophy, Hokmah, Shekina, and Gaia. I gave It (Her) a name because, to me, She was a living, breathing presence—as alive to me as any person I've ever met. As strange as it may sound, She "talked" to me and calmed my fears. Now, a decade later, I still feel this Power and Presence in my life, more continually and more deeply than ever. But it is without gender now, and far less dramatic. In truth, it feels quite ordinary. It simply *is*.

Here again, your experience may be very different from mine. Just as you will find your wilderness in your own place, you will have your own experience of Presence there. But my guess is that you will be touched and moved by *Something* that is in you but yet not completely you, something dynamic, surprising, and very, very wise.

I would also bet that if you are willing, and if you listen very gently and carefully, you will sense that this mysterious Wisdom is ready to lead you, guide you to where you need to be. It is your wilderness calling.

THE WISDOM OF WILDERNESS

One
THE CALL

. . . to the mountain and to the hill,
to where the pure water flows,
and further, deep into the thicket . . .
—SAINT JOHN OF THE CROSS, *SPIRITUAL CANTICLE*

FIRST TRIP TO THE MOUNTAIN

Summer, 1990. I'm on my way. The miles are going quickly now that I'm on the interstate with the metropolitan traffic behind me. I'm driving through hilly green countryside feeling very much alive. I notice my mind shifting from thoughts about things left undone to excitement and wonder about what I'm getting into.

I relax a little. My hands loosen on the steering wheel and I'm aware now of how tight my shoulder muscles have been. How long has this tension been in me? Certainly for months, perhaps

1

even years. I smell the canvas of my old, long-unused pup tent in the back of the car. It's hot and I've been driving with the windows up and the air-conditioning on. *Ease it*, I think.

I don't know what that means, but it has something to do with the ancient tension in my shoulders, a tightness I'm so used to I don't usually feel it. I turn off the air-conditioning and roll down the windows and the warm airstream hits my face and blows my hair and I roll my neck a little. Something relaxing is happening and I love it, every bit of the feeling of it inside me. I feel love, almost romantic love for the smell of the old pup tent, love for the air messing up my hair, love for being here on this interstate. Then I see the mountains.

The Allegheny foothills always surprise me. I've traveled this interstate many times, coming up out of the Piedmont Plateau, and it's always the same: I'm driving along and the hills are not there, then suddenly, even when I know where to expect them, they appear as if they had just decided to show up. A surprise of beauty. As I see them now, though, I sense more than their beauty; it's a deep homecoming, welcoming feeling. I could swear the mountains are reaching out for me, as if they have palpable arms opening, guiding, ready to take me in. Everything in me relaxes at this. I want to be taken in. I am overcome with love, right here on the interstate, passing a tractor trailer, its diesel roaring into the wind in a great rushing whine. I'm not anywhere near the State Forest yet, but I've said Yes to a call, and I've been taken. I'm in love.

The call of wilderness is very familiar to me. In one way or another, it is probably always calling. Sometimes I have felt it inwardly as an old, familiar longing, a passion unfulfilled—what Thoreau called a "yearning for the Wild" that no language could ever express.[1] At its most powerful, however, the call seemed to have come from outside me, from some wild place and Presence—a true "call of the wild." The image that comes to me is of a mountain forest opening invisible arms to me, inviting me to enter into its secret places so deeply and completely that I finally disappear—and there, in soft, rich lostness, I will be healed; my own true nature will be restored. It is a familiar feeling.

Although I do not recall the beginnings of this feeling, I know it is very old. Its roots go far back in my life, their fibers touching my earliest memories: sunlight on my crib, the sacred sound and touch of raindrops, the smells of dusty fields and musty forests where I was carried by my parents, the tender brushing of breezes upon my skin.

A full memory comes. I am very young, no more than four years old. My father has taken me hunting with him. It is not the first time I have come with him, and I am proud that he brings me along. My little legs are keeping up with his strides, my small hand in his, and I feel the soft happy crunch of our walking across the hayfield in late autumn, the afternoon sun just at the top of the tree line, his wool shirt rough like his hand and his whiskery cheeks, and there is no trace of fear in my body.

I walk on his right side as always, while in the crook of his left arm he carries his twelve-gauge, double-barreled Ithaca Featherweight shotgun, its breech open so the gun bends to fit the curve of his elbow like a part of him. Our little springer spaniel—dear God, I wish I could remember his name—nuzzles into a brush pile up ahead and suddenly stops still. My father releases my hand and I too become still, like the dog is still, like the air, like the whole world. My father whispers, softer than breath, lips with a slight grin and barely moving, "Dog never points."

In the stillness I hear the click of the breech closing. It is a soft sound, and I love it because it is gentle and I know another sound will be coming soon, an explosion so huge and harsh that it will overwhelm me no matter how completely I expect it. Yet there is no fear anywhere, no tension, only stillness inside and out. My father steps forward once, twice, casually, not prowling, just loose, easy. I stay still. I know it is my job to remain motionless, though I do not recall my father ever teaching me so. The dog sees my father moving and moves forward also, and suddenly a giant part of the brush flops and flaps upward screaming for the air, trying to get there and the sound of the shotgun nearly knocks me over and in the after-ringing with my hands too late over my ears I hear, "Nice bird. You got you a nice pheasant, Jerry." He has turned and is smiling big at me and for some reason so cloudy to me now, I feel very proud of myself. I smile big back.

My father is already walking toward the brush pile where I know something is lying and I hope it is lying very still and really dead. "Fetch," he calls to the dog. Turning back to me he laughs. "Dog won't fetch. Lookit him." Indeed, the dog is standing still, unable or unwilling to search out the bird. Like the dog, I don't want to go where the bird lies. This is my first fear, the beginning of tenseness in my body. I don't want the bird to be not dead. I know my father does not like it when a bird is wounded. I know I do not like it. I don't even want to watch the dog for fear he will again flush the wounded bird and it will struggle up once more, splattering blood with no hope for the sky. But I do watch, carefully, for if it happens I must see it. Is this my first courage? Or the beginning of morbid allure? All I know is that fear—and the dissipation of it—made me part of the natural world, made me feel alive.

My father moves into the high grass, laughing because now the dog decides to come in from the side. "Yeah, now you'll get it, won't you?" my father chuckles. I smile a little, still conscious of the unseen bird, perhaps not dead. My father laughs again. "Well, go ahead. Get it. Fetch." At his words the dog stops again and blinks dumbly at my father, who now doubles over with laughter. Then the dog sits, as if waiting for my father to collect himself, and this strikes my father as so hilarious that he lays the shotgun in the grass and lays himself in the grass and holds his stomach and laughs himself into tears with his legs in the air, wonderful huge laughs echoing off the tree line, healing the field and the sky and all my fear. I run giggling to him and leap onto his stomach and he doesn't see me coming and I knock his breath away. He grabs me and we're rolling in the grass and the dog leaps in and there's nothing in the universe but laughter and tumbling and hay straws down my back. Then we lie holding our stomachs, recovering under the merciful sky as the tree shadows reach us and a breeze begins. "Well, Jerry," says my father, "let's get your bird."

I don't remember whether the bird was alive or dead. I like to think it was completely dead, a clean shot. I do remember walking home, my father carrying the pheasant until we got near the house because it was too heavy for me, then giving it to me and I was so proud in the early dark to show my mother what we had brought for dinner. I remember the sleekness and rich colors of the feathers and later the hard deep taste of the meat, and the need to watch out for shot buried in the flesh that could break a tooth if you bit down too hard. I was very small.

NEVER ALONE

Like most sons, I'm sure I idolize my father in many ways, but he really was an expert outdoorsman. He was a professional. He built camps for churches and the YMCA, and during the Depression he made a living leading fishing trips to Isle Royale and on up into Canada. I remember stories he told of the businessmen he had guided into the north woods, men who still had enough money to make such a trip, men who were longing to escape the stress of hard times, men who had become so stony-hard themselves they were ready to crack like the thin, cold skipping rocks you find along winter lakeshores that break when you try to pick them out of the frozen sand. "Softening up" was what my father said happened to the men on those trips. Just being out there, everyone would become increasingly silly and wild and natural. My father would grin as he described how deeply the men loved being softened up and how they didn't even know it was happening to them.

I remember my father hunting, fishing, camping, walking

through woods among birches and sweet pines, rowing his wooden boat out into small Michigan lakes where gentle waves collected foam and made luffing sounds on the shore where I stood in the morning, watching. I don't remember his ever teaching me about the outdoors. I don't recall his saying a single word about how to build a fire or pitch a tent, but just by watching him I learned something more important—his way of being there.

His way of being outdoors was very different from that of my mother. She came from a family of farmers who saw all of nature—including human nature—as an adversary, something to be tamed. In contrast, my father's family were teachers, preachers, and shopkeepers. The wonderful thing about their attitude toward nature was that they didn't have one—they just spent time there. They made no comments about it.

As I look back now from my own unchosen physical vulnerability, I am touched by how vulnerable my father was in the outdoors, how very unprotected. Time after time he would come home hurt in some way, scratched by thorns or covered with poison oak or mosquito bites, or shivering blue from cold, or green from seasickness because the wind had come up on the lake. My mother always huffed about what he should have done to avoid such dangers, but he never took her advice. He went his own way, following his own call.

He died when I was nine. It wasn't untimely; he was an old man even when I was born. But if he had lived longer, I think he might have shown me something more about being alone in the wild. As it was, I grew up under my mother's almost paranoid protectiveness and I never went out alone overnight. There were, according to her, too many dangers. I went to church and scout camps, went fishing with friends, learned how to build a fire and pitch a tent, but I never went out overnight alone.

In later years, I did a lot of family camping with my wife and young children. Still under the influence of my mother's paranoia about the wilderness, I took on the responsibility of ensuring my family's safety. I was very organized about camping, making lists of all potential dangers and taking every possible precaution. Often I would become ponderously obsessive about details, but my family put up with me in much the same way they put up with bugs and poison ivy.

I guess I can take some credit for our having had no serious accidents. Everyone remained safe, and all six of us, Betty and myself, Earl, Paul, Greg, and little Julie, had great fun. Over the years we accumulated a treasure of family photographs and memories: the fresh Canadian sand dunes along Lake Huron, the smooth wet rocks of Lake Superior's shores, the dry spaciousness and unending sky of southwestern deserts, the high thin cold of Yosemite, the bugs and soggy heat of the Gulf of Mexico, the cool beauty of a coral reef out of Key Largo, where a delighted Julie screeched "Fersh! Fersh!" right through her little snorkel. It was all fine, truly family fine. But I never went out alone overnight.

There came a time when the kids were teenagers and Betty was high-gear into her own career, and the family camping stopped. Occasionally the kids would still go fishing with me—I had inherited my father's addiction to fishing—but most of the time they wanted to do their own things with their own friends. For a while I went out with a couple of my adult friends, one of whom had a Jeep. We'd drive through the forest over dirt roads, go fishing, drink a couple of beers, and have wonderful, dazed weekends. Eventually, though, my friends moved away. I still wanted to be out there, but it was at the point where, if I were going to do it at all, I would have to do it alone.

THE FOREST

In the fall of 1987 my old car broke down and I bought a little Chevy Blazer with four-wheel drive. This brought the kids—the boys at least; Julie never quite got into it—temporarily back into my outdoor fold. They and their friends loved going off-road, especially in the snow. We were always looking for new places to go four-wheeling, places where we wouldn't get arrested or do too much damage to the landscape. We spent a lot of time grinding through the mud of construction sites, where the novelty wore off quickly. Then, finally, when the boys were otherwise occupied, I began to go alone, just driving.

One day Chris, a friend of my sons (who, over the years, has become another son to me), gave me a crumpled copy of a newspaper article about the Green Ridge State Forest in the Appalachian Mountains, not too far from our home. "Looks like a good place to go four-wheelin'," he said. The article described miles of trails accessible only with four-wheel drive. I thanked him and filed the article.

The article sat in my files for two years while I sank into my work and, barely knowing it, into midlife. It was a time of losses and hidden births of freedoms. My mother died, friendships broke up, my work became routine. I felt the first signs of aging in my body and began to wonder what life yet held for me—and what I might have missed. Julie was having trouble in school. I felt grief for many things, including perhaps the first true grief over my father's death. All the while, my spiritual life was deepening, drawing me increasingly toward some kind of intimate in-the-moment guidance by the Divine. I felt an increasing need for solitude. The children were young adults and I'd finished writing my seventh book, the one I said was "the last one I really needed to write." I felt more free than ever, but as is so often the case with newborn freedom, it was deeply tinged with sadness.

Through it all, I was feeling an increasingly passionate yearning for . . . something. I called it my longing for God, and of course that's what all our deepest longings really are, but I could just as well have said it was a longing for love, for union, for fully being in life, for being vitally connected with everything. It was always with me; nothing satisfied it, and sometimes—quite frequently, in fact—it seemed unbearable. This particular yearning, I now know, had been with me all my life. It was the power behind my striving, the reason for my ambition, the need that fired all the energies of my life. It was my eros, my passion, my relentlessness of spirit.

By the early summer of 1990, the yearning had become increasingly conscious and insistent. Somehow it connected with the wilderness, and finally, inexplicably, with the state forest in the article that Chris had given me. One day, barely aware of what I was doing, I dug out the old clipping and called the phone number it gave. The number still worked and the ranger who answered said, "Sure, you can come on up here. We got lots of campsites. They're primitive, you know. No facilities. Gotta bring your own water and stuff. No bathrooms. A few picnic tables, but that's it. Can't even hunt now . . . nothing's in season."

"No, no hunting. I just want to get away, be alone for a while."

"Well, this is a good place to do it. This time of year you're likely not to see another human being. Nobody's here when it's not hunting season. Come on up anytime."

"What's your fee for camping?"

"Nothing. No fee. You gotta register, though."

I knew I was going.

My old obsessiveness struck as I planned for the trip. I began making lists. Although the prospect of going out alone overnight beckoned me with unutterable sweetness, I was also afraid. The fear made me careful, and carefulness made me obsessive, and at certain points the obsessiveness became paranoia. In my lists I considered not only what I'd need for food and shelter, but all the dangers I might encounter. I thought about wasps and spiders, poison ivy and twisted ankles, floods and fires and copperheads and black bears and packs of wild dogs.

Most of all, I regretted that I had ever seen the movie *Deliverance*. I could prepare for poison ivy and be watchful about animals, but there was nothing I could do about malevolent drunken good old boys. Unless I had a gun. I actually thought about a gun. I, the guy who got banned from helicopter flights in Vietnam because I refused to carry a sidearm, the man who, after returning from

Vietnam, got rid of the dear old Ithaca Featherweight double-barreled shotgun I had inherited from my father—I was actually considering a gun.

At that point I realized I had crossed the line into paranoia. The idea of a gun seemed so wrong, so opposed to the yearning that called me. Suddenly all my other plans for forestalling dangers began to feel wrong as well. I remember the moment: I was sitting cross-legged on the floor of my study, surrounded by camping gear, my list in my hand, when the feeling of wrongness came to me. I closed my eyes, took a breath, tried to pray a little. In that moment I had my first vague sense of the mountain forest *welcoming* me, a gentle, utterly soft openness of invitation, a tender hospitality. In that sweet atmosphere, my paranoia seemed an insult, a slap in the face, a door slammed shut against the mountain's offered embrace. I laid the list on the floor beside me and the feeling of wrongness disappeared. In its place was an equally powerful sense of rightness. *I know enough about camping,* I thought. *I don't need any more lists. When it's time, I'll just pack up and go.*

Two weeks later I packed up and went. I couldn't resist making just one list for the absolute necessities: food, tent, sleeping bag, and the like. But I didn't become paranoid, and when a little obsessiveness would begin to creep in, I simply took a breath. I had been looking forward to the trip for a couple of weeks, and as I took care of final details at home and office, I felt like a child inside, jumping with expectancy. I remember marveling at my excitement, not sure what I thought was going to be so wonderful. I wasn't really expecting anything specific. The excitement was the simple feeling of rightness in responding to a call I had ignored for a very long time.

I suppose you can tell that something is really right when you feel such a sense of interior exuberance, of "Oh, yes. This is it!" I know there's more to spiritual discernment than good feelings, but if the exuberance goes deep enough, it doesn't matter what your rational mind has to say about it. It's like a homecoming, something lost being found, a feeling that makes your insides shimmer with rightness. And if you don't say yes to it, you yourself feel wrong, and a little less alive.

Two

THE POWER OF
THE SLOWING

*There you will show me
what my soul has been seeking . . .*

—SAINT JOHN OF THE CROSS, *SPIRITUAL CANTICLE*

As I drive into the Appalachian foothills, a little obsessiveness comes to me; I filled the tank with gas, but I don't think I checked the tires. What if I get a flat up in the mountains and my spare doesn't have enough air? I pull into a gas station and check. Everything's fine. Back on the road, I am a little ashamed for the worry. But it was a reasonable concern and I had become only just a tiny bit paranoid. I smile. I realize now that I'm starting to guard against obsessiveness; I'm trying not to be paranoid, and somehow *that* doesn't seem right. For God's sake, I don't want to obsess about becoming obsessive, be paranoid about getting paranoid. I take a grinning breath. A prayer comes. "God, I don't know what you want. Hell, I don't even know what *I* want. But I want to want what you want. I just want to be available, open, for . . . whatever."

I relax again as I drive on into the mountain forest's arms, feeling an encircling warmth, more, more. The closer I get to the State Forest, the stronger the welcoming becomes. I feel it like a caress, and I sense myself responding to it, wanting to be welcoming myself, wanting to gently enter gentleness, desiring to be as hospitable to the wilderness as it is to me. Somewhere on the final road the words actually come: "The Power of the Slowing."

It is a naming, and the name is absolutely right. What I am experiencing is exactly the Power of the Slowing, yet I have no idea what it means. I cannot get my mind around it—and that also feels absolutely right. It mystifies me, and I am further mystified by my enjoyment of being mystified. Here's something I am feeling so strongly, and I don't understand it at all. And I don't need to—a great relief for a psychiatrist. I have been beautifully, exquisitely mystified.

By the time I reach the rangers' office I am lightheaded, as though from fasting or breathing rarefied air. It seems to have something to do with not thinking, freedom from my usual figuring-out, strategizing, organizing, comprehending. My mind has simply quit such things. They just aren't happening. I don't remember ever feeling so free, but I don't really care about that either. All I know is there's confidence in this moment, lightness inside and out. I have been slowed down. I have been slowed by a Power.

As I turn off the ignition and get out of the car I am pleased, simply pleased by the smell of the air, the brown wood of the rangers' office, the green of trees, the fact that there are no other cars in the parking lot.

Inside the Green Ridge office, feeling almost drunk, I say to the ranger, "I'd like a campsite."

He smiles. "Sure 'nuff. Where you want?"

I pause.

"You been here before?"

"No."

"Well, here's a map. You can have your pick today. Don't get many folks out here except hunting season. Nobody else right now. What ya gonna be doin'?"

"Nothing. Maybe a little hiking. I'm just looking for some solitude. What would you choose if you wanted to get away from everything?"

"You really want to get way back in?"

"Yes."

Some little place in the back of my mind is smiling. Maybe that's what I've always been seeking: a way back in. Yes.

"You got four-wheel?"

"Yep." I say it casually, manly.

He pulls the map toward him, thinking. His finger touches one site, then another, finally lights on a third. "Here's a good one. Way back in. Lotta privacy. You might like that."

"Okay. Sign me up."

The ranger draws directions for me on the map and then I'm back in the car, tracing the map, tracking dusty lanes through miles of forest. I see no cars, no hunters, no one. The farther I go, the more difficult it is to follow the roads, and the roads curve around mountain cliffs, and I am beginning to feel a little anxiety. Have I gotten into more wildness than I'd bargained for? Then, as if it were an immediate response to my concern, I am moved to stop the car. I turn off the ignition, set the brake, and get out and just stand, looking at the trees, the mountainside, the sky. The welcoming feeling is here again, powerfully reassuring, holding me. I am bathed in a quality that is nothing other than friendliness. It comes with such deep soft strength and the name comes again: the Power of the Slowing. It seems to be renewing itself for me, in me, all around me. Again I respond, feeling my own deep friendliness, my own hospitality. I am in love, but I don't know with what or with whom. Just in love.

Dirt road turns into rocky lane, into bare track, up a little rise where I have to kick in the four-wheel drive, back into a clearing where a weathered picnic table stands next to a fire pit circled by stones. I turn off the engine and the silence overwhelms me. Stillness now, not a breeze, not a breath, a silence thick like a blanket, a quilt of no-sound.

SLOWING

I am still sitting behind the wheel when my mind suddenly erupts with ideas of things to do. Get the tent out, set up camp, light a fire, get everything arranged so I can start enjoying myself. The impulses are almost desperate, as if my mind has awakened startled, terrified by its own depth of peacefulness, abruptly afraid of dying from inaction. I respond immediately. I have the car door open, my foot on the ground, ready to unpack, when I am simply stopped by something. I feel it within me, inside my very muscles, yet it seems to come from somewhere outside me. It is not me, yet it is rising from the deepest part of me. It is powerful, as if a great gentle hand has taken my arms and legs and simply stilled them, and a sweet irresistible voice is speaking in my belly, "Be still now." It's not a real voice, not actual hearing, but the message is clear: no rush, no need to do anything, just be.

One foot on the ground, one hand still on the open car door, I relax back into the driver's seat. Slowed. My impulse had been to rush out of the car and start setting up camp, but the slowing has stopped me. Now I simply am. I sit half in, half out of the car for a long time, but I no longer know anything about time. I don't know anything about anything. I sense the smell of the woods, the caress of the mountain breeze, the spots of warmth where sunlight touches me through high leaves and branches, the soft feeling of my muscles relaxing. I have no notion of being perceptive or alert, but the depth of my relaxation has made me very open, receptive to everything. Again the welcoming feeling comes, the friendliness, and now, just now it does seem to be time to unload the car.

BUGS

It is midafternoon. The sun is hot, the air still. I'm taking things out of the car and piling them on the old picnic table. I set the water jug down and a few drops leak out and bead on the rough wood, and yellow jackets arrive from nowhere. I am used to these little wasps hovering over picnic lunches at home, but I did not expect them here on the mountain. I am disappointed to see them—I think they will be a problem. Thinking starts, my mind revs up; I begin to cope. I consider putting on some insect repellent, but something slows my thoughts again and the friendliness-feeling returns. I go on unpacking. As I put my box of food on the picnic table, horseflies appear, mixing with the yellow jackets, buzzing and humming, black and yellow. I sit down and watch them. I pour a little puddle of water on the table. Two yellow jackets alight there and drink. They seem so vulnerable in this moment, their tiny heads bent to the water.

More bugs come, flying, buzzing, hovering, crawling. I do not like their presence at all, but the friendliness-feeling keeps coming in waves and I just sit with them. A yellow jacket lands on my right arm, a horsefly on my left. I want to brush them off, but again I am slowed. I wait. They crawl on my arms, looking for droplets of sweat, not tickling me, just touching. I hear cicadas singing. I realize they've been droning all along, but I haven't noticed them until now. Now I hear the sounds of now.

I continue setting up camp and the bugs keep hovering. The sun has moved to shine directly on me and I'm sweating with the work, feeling wonderful. I take off my shirt, hang it on a branch, feel the sunshine on my back. Occasionally a bug crawls on my skin and tickles and I twitch a little and it flies away.

In my arms I now hold the old pup tent, unopened for years. I smell its canvas mustiness in the sunlight. I do not think, but rather sense where it should go, what direction it should face. Like the timing of things, the placement of things is just given. It seems right. I am barefoot and in my shorts now, kneeling in the dirt and small sharp rocks, clearing a place for the tent. It occurs to me that I have never felt this way before, never so fully here, never so completely now.

The site is cleared, the tent ready to set up, but I pause. Finally, it seems to be a time for thinking. I pull a can of beer from the cooler and sit in the dirt against a tree. I rub the skin of my back against the bark of the tree, gentle, close, good. My mind is gentle too, and the thoughts that come are free. All drivenness is gone. No agendas or plans arise. Just easy reflection. No, I have never felt this way before. But wait, is there not some small memory of it from long ago, some vague sense of familiarity? No, I guess not. If it is a memory, it must be from long before my sense of me—maybe even from before my birth. I sip the cold beer.

I remember past times of camping, old ways of setting up tents, sighting the ground and figuring out level places and which direction the tent door should face and where water would run if it rained, and making sure everything got set up before dark, all strategies and tactics, procedures and plans. How different it is now, just following what seems right, going where something opens, responding to what is given. I am letting myself be guided; I have been empowered to respond to tender, subtle senses of direction. I have agreed to the empowering. I, or my heart, has said yes. I have wanted it. My mind now begins to work a little: how does this guidance happen, where is it coming from? But a gentle slowing hand stills the impulse. I take another swallow of beer, lean back more fondly against the tree. Maybe I doze off a little. Cicadas drone. Horseflies and yellow jackets come and go, tickle, touch, buzz, and disappear.

The tent, it turns out, is the last thing to set up. The sun has gone below the tops of the trees and leaf shadows shimmer on the blue-green canvas as I unfold it. It takes just two poles, one at each end. Long ago I lost the original aluminum poles, and what I have now is broken broomsticks. They don't really fit, but it doesn't matter. I tie the canvas to the sticks with string. Good enough. I walk to the car to get my sleeping bag and smile. It's not there. I laugh aloud and the forest stills slightly at the sound. I had made my list, made sure the sleeping bag was on it, but I didn't put the sleeping bag in the car. Well, what's here is just a thin old blanket jammed behind the spare tire. Okay, it will have to do. I shake it out, refold it, start to crawl into the tent with it.

I'm halfway into the tent when a blazing pain hits my back. I scream and scuttle backward, out and up and trying to reach the place in the middle of my back just beneath my shoulder blades and impossible to get to, but I do touch something soft that falls. On the ground, crawling dazedly, is a yellow jacket. God I hate that bug. I would stomp it if I weren't barefoot. My back is on fire. Oh Jesus, the thing was riding on my back and I squeezed it against the canvas as I crawled into the tent. Did I squash it? The pain is easing now as I kneel on the earth and look at the crawling insect. "You're in worse shape than I am," I say to it. "Your wings don't work."

My mind starts again. What the hell am I doing, out here in the middle of nowhere half-naked on my knees whispering sweetnesses to a damn bug that's just stung my back where I can't even touch it?

The Power of the Slowing comes again now, like a wave of warmth inside me, and this time She is laughing, and She fills me with laughter, and the bug, I imagine, knows nothing of laughter. And I realize, quite suddenly, that I have just called the Power of the Slowing "She."

SHE

That first trip to the mountain was full of surprises. Never before had I felt such a sense of a living Presence not my own. Never had I felt so clearly drawn and guided by something beyond my own will. And with all that, I was absolutely certain the Presence was feminine.

I've thought about it a lot. I considered that the whole experience might be my own creation. It began in a midlife time when I had suffered losses and was under stress. Could my psyche be kicking up its Jungian heels and manufacturing a disembodied woman-sense to meet some unconscious need? I could never say for certain. All I know is that when I experienced the Power of the Slowing, it was as real, as substantial as anything I had ever perceived. Even my sense of Her as feminine was more like a direct observation than an interpretation. She simply was who She was.

The piercing thing for me was not that the Presence was feminine, but that She showed up at all. My best psychological insight is that without really knowing it, I had been looking for that kind of Presence all my life. I remember feeling connected with everything around me when I was a very small child. The trees, sky, and sun and all of nature were not only friendly; they were in some way part of me, or I a part of them. That was before I had to set myself apart and become a boy who was learning things *about* the world. Somehow, learning about the world made me feel separate from it, and I had been longing for reconnection ever since.

From the time I was five or six until I became a teenager, Jesus—or, rather, my image of Jesus—was my way of reconnecting. Sunday school had presented Jesus as someone who was actually around somewhere in our lives, hidden from sight but very involved, loving children and animals and all creation. I prayed to him often, had fantasies of walking and talking with him, took him into my little heart as best I could. But as young as I was, I still realized that my contact with Jesus was pretty much a result of my own interpretations. *And he never actually showed up.* My physical eyes never saw what the eyes of my imagination did: a real Jesus walking, smiling across a meadow toward me. I never felt the physical touch of his arm around my shoulder. I wanted that. I wanted to be reconnected, not just through images and beliefs but sensibly, palpably. I wanted direct experience.

Before the encounter with the Power of the Slowing, I had had many experiences of what I would call Divine Presence, but they were always indirect, what the theologians call *mediated*. I felt the Great Mystery through the birth of my children, through the love of my wife and family and friends, through the beauty of sunsets and music. I sensed grace abounding in people: in their healing, growing, choosing love, finding their ways. I had more of a sense of the goodness of things than any man deserves, and yet I wasn't satisfied.

To my mind, all these experiences were *evidences* of the Divine Presence, *signs* of grace, *results* of God's goodness, all once removed from their Source. The experiences were encouraging and inspiring, but not fulfilling. They all carried the message that reconnection is possible, but they did not actually connect me. They tantalized, teased, even tortured me by fanning the flames of my longing for direct encounter. Many around me said I should be satisfied with what I had, for I had been given so much. But I could not help my desire. I could not make peace with seeing through a glass darkly when I yearned for face-to-face Presence. My cup overflowed with mediated experience, yet I thirsted for the *im*mediate.

So it was that She showed up. She whispered, beckoned, called from the mountain forest that was to be the home of my encounter with Her, demanding that I come alone and vulnerable. She wanted me willing and wild enough to meet Her in Her wildness. I was in need of healing and She had so much to teach me, so many places to guide me, so many gifts to give me. But most of all She wanted what I wanted: for me to sense Her Presence directly. She wanted me to feel Her touch on and in my body as palpably as I felt the hard ground on my bare knees or the tree bark on my back or the sting of the yellow jacket beneath my shoulder blades. She wanted me to feel Her hand stilling my muscles, Her Power in my belly, Her guiding Wisdom in my heart. That is why She came.

Three
NIGHT FEAR

Oh Guiding night!
Oh night more lovely than the dawn!

—SAINT JOHN OF THE CROSS, *THE DARK NIGHT*

The bugs left with the evening breeze, and the ending of the day was filled with unbelievable sweetness. My eyes were new and soft as I watched the dusk come in, the summer sun moving down behind the western tree line, and all things gentling in subtle twilight incandescence. I don't think I had ever before really *seen* the sun set, been with it so steadily and intimately as it disappeared. It was as if it were my very first sunset, and I felt a little sadness at its end.

In the tenderness of twilight I built a fire. I had meant to cook a big dinner, but the fire itself captured my attention. I savored the fire as I had savored the sunset, noticing how the breeze kept changing its shape, the way the flames transformed each twig into blazing light, into glowing ember, into white ash. The fire hypnotized me and I saw things in it, soft curvatures of light and heat that moved into my awareness and caressed places in me, places that were hurt and hardened, places of grief, of old woundings and wonderings. There, deep inside me, the touches of the fire-curves were like tender fingers, deeply good. It was my first solitude fire and I named it "Healing Fire." The name came to me in the same way "The Power of the Slowing" had come, out of nowhere into my mind. I was suddenly aware that, as I watched the sun set and as I built the fire, I had thought about nothing at all. The words *Healing Fire* were the first to come into my mind in what must have been several hours. I offered a little prayer of thanksgiving, wordlessly.

I must have cooked and eaten something that first evening, but I don't remember it. All I recall is the sunset, and how the fire entranced and healed me, and how, when my eyes finally left the fire, night had fully come. I looked into the surrounding trees and saw only blackness. I moved closer to the fire, as if it offered protection from something. Suddenly the fire seemed very important to me. Without thought or image or sound, without any cause, I was afraid. The fear just came, changing the texture of my awareness almost softly, like the breeze changed the shape of the flames.

BEAR

I think I might stay here by this fire all night. I can feed it, keep it burning high. But I am so tired now. Whatever time it is, it is time to sleep. I look toward my tent and barely see it. It will take a little courage to go over there and crawl in. Courage is good. There will be no fear in the morning, and now, though I am afraid, it is time to sleep.

I get up and slowly follow the beam of my flashlight into the night, away from the fire, legs stiff from long sitting, walking slowly across the campsite that has been my home this day but now in the darkness seems alien, unmapped. It is cold. I go to the car and pull out a sweater, chuckling again about having forgotten my sleeping bag. A strange feeling, this laughter while I am afraid. It reminds me somehow of carbonation, of bubbles in water.

I try to make my mind work: think of things to take care of before getting into the tent. Something in my mind doesn't care that I'm avoiding sleep as long as possible. Think about bears. Get all the food and cooking utensils away from the tent. Put them in the car, put the garbage in the car, close it up. Just a canteen of water, maybe a beer in the tent. Might a bear be thirsty? Do bears like beer? Bears are nothing to be afraid of anyway, not the ones around here. What else might be a danger in the night? Nothing I can think of, really. I suppose a snake might have crawled into the tent as the evening chill came; I'll look around in there. But nothing else. Nothing real, nothing even imagined.

Sometimes you just take your chances. My mind grows philosophical as I stand in the chill by the car in the night. There's a sort of freedom when you've done what you can do and you just have to give up and let be. It's not a matter of trust; it's simply that there's nothing else left to do. Someone said courage is fear that has said its prayers. I guess my prayers have been said, said without thinking, back there in the fire's entrancement before I saw the dark. Perhaps this thing I feel now as I stand in the night is the raw nature of courage. I realize I no longer know the difference between fear and courage. They are made of the same stuff. Maybe courage just has a little extra choice in it. Right now my choice is very simple: stand here all night or get into the damn tent.

Kneeling on the ground, I open the tent flap and explore inside with my flashlight for snakes, bugs, whatever else might be in here. *Nothing. Did I check everywhere? What are you really looking for, Jerry? Forget it; you're making yourself paranoid again.* I look back into the darkness. There are no stars, no moon, just night. The fire is almost out. I could put on another log, stay with it just a little while, but I truly am too tired. It is time. I crawl into the tent, feet first, zip up the flap, wrap my blanket around me. The ground is hard and I am already cold. It is all right. Everything is all right. Maybe I could keep my flashlight on and read for a while or write in my journal? No, I'm just looking for something more to do and my eyes are gritty from fatigue and fire-smoke. I let them close, and I hear, for the first time, the small vague sounds of the night. I do not know what they are, these soft whirrings and whooshings and cracklings, but they are almost comforting. I am not alone. I'm not really sure now; perhaps I'd rather be alone.

I lie awake for a long time, sleepy yet energized by fear. I realize the fear is just happening, all by itself. Nothing is scaring me. It's not that I have an idea about what might be of danger and then become afraid of it. It's the fear-feeling itself that comes, and then my mind looks for something to be afraid of. Rustling leaves, the snap of a twig breaking, what is it? Or who? Some small creature moving, a skunk, a possum, who knows or cares? It's too still now, and the tiny sounds crack the silence, make me jump, my heart beat fast. Nothing more to do. Just sleep. *Please God let me sleep now, because there's nothing more to do.*

I sleep and dream. I dream that a car drives up into my campsite, its headlights bearing down on my pup tent, closer and closer until I am awake. I'm not sure it really was a dream. I think I smell exhaust fumes. I sleep again, dreaming of sounds, snappings and whirrings and then a growling that awakens me and I am certain the growl has come from a close wild presence that is just a few inches from me, just on the other side of the thin shadow canvas of the tent. I am sharp awake now and smell something right here, a brusque, wild smell, the smell of some-thing alive and very near. I lie still, nostrils open to the smell, ears sharp into the silence, eyes keen into absolute darkness, and it growls again.

The bear is right next to me, its side brushing the tent canvas, its growl deep, resonant, slow. This is no dream and I am terri-fied and yet I feel a strange calmness over everything, so difficult to describe. It's like some kind of fierce embrace. I lie absolutely still, staring wide-eyed at nothing. My mind appears, thinking fast. What do you do to get rid of a bear? I heard somewhere you bang pots and pans together. *Okay. Do I have any pots and pans? No, dummy, you put them in the car with the food so they wouldn't attract bears. Okay. Okay. So there's nothing to do, still nothing to do. Still nothing. Lie here, still, be scared, nothing more to do.* And here, maybe, another deeper voice, just a hint of a touch of the Power of the Slowing whisper-ing, "Be frightened. Just be frightened."

The bear paws at something, ambles toward the picnic table, comes back once around the other side of the tent. And leaves. Just like that. A patrol through my campsite with no wasted motion. No more growls. Nothing. My back and legs hurt from the cold hard ground and from keeping still. My heart is beating so loudly I'm sure the bear must hear it. And I have never felt so alive.

I lie unmoving for a very long time after the bear leaves, my senses completely alert, no thoughts, no images, seeing nothing, hearing only my heart and breath and the sounds of the night. For the first time in my life, I am experiencing pure fear. I am completely present in it, in a place beyond all coping because there is nothing to do. I have never before experienced such clean, unadulterated purity of emotion. This fear is naked. It consists, in these slowly passing moments, of my heart pounding, my breath rushing yet fully silent, my body ready for anything, my mind absolutely empty, open, waiting. I *am* fear. It is beautiful.

PURITY

Once I saw a deer like that: a deer made of pure fear. I was sitting on a rock in the woods when I heard crashing crushing sounds coming toward me. A group of five or six deer was running before two wild dogs. As the deer approached, they veered off to their left, away from me, but one, smaller than the others and lagging behind them, kept straight toward me. It was nearly upon me when it froze, catching my scent I presume, and was for a moment motionless.

In that instant, the little deer was nothing but complete, perfect deer fear. It simply *was* terror, eyes wide round white, mouth gaping drooling, nostrils wide steaming, muscles shimmering in sweated fur. It looked left and right—not, I think, deciding where to go, but simply, nakedly *seeing* with complete absence of intent—and then it ran, crashing through the brush after its mates. The dogs came then, silent, smooth, silky deadly, disappearing over the wooded hillside after their prey.

In the tent that night, lying still as a dead man while the bear brushed next to me, I was fear like that deer, so pure, perfection. How can I describe my sense of the privilege of feeling so impeccably afraid and my supreme gratitude for it?

After the bear left, I rolled slowly onto my stomach, found my flashlight, opened the tent flap, and sent the light beam across the campsite to the surrounding trees. Nothing there.

Wobbly and breathless all at once, I crawled out of the tent and stood, took a few unsteady steps to where I could lean against a tree, unbuttoned my fly. When I had finished I looked up and there, beyond the branches, completely unexpected, were hundreds of thousands of stars, a night brilliance so overwhelming I fell back against the tree, grasping for it, not to keep from falling but to stay on earth. "Thank you, God," I whispered into the radiant night.

GRATITUDE

I am not completely certain what I was saying thank you for. It wasn't just for the star-beauty, nor for surviving the bear experience.

It seemed to be for the privilege of being alive in the totality of everything, the gift of fully existing right then and there. Fear, like any other strong emotion, can make you exquisitely conscious of living, perfectly aware of being in the moment. It can only do that, however, on those rare occasions when you don't try to fight it, run away from it, cope with it, suppress it, tame it, or otherwise domesticate it. The real gift of that night was that I had been unable to do anything about my fear of the bear. Lying there in the tent, I could not run away; I could not make the bear go away; I could not reassure myself that things were going to be all right; I could not trick my mind into thinking about something else. There was nothing to be done, and that was the gift. I could only be there in the real situation, being real, being pure fear. That is why, I think, that after the bear left, as I grabbed that sweet tree under the stars, I became pure gratitude.

That lesson has served me well over the years. There have been so many times now that I could have tried to fight my fear but instead have somehow been empowered just to be in it. I am also humbled by how much of my previous life I had spent trying to tame fear and other emotions, keeping them under control, civilizing them. I knew no better, but I still grieve a little over how much of my life-energy I stifled in that process.

In my psychiatric practice how many times did I help patients cope with their feelings, tame the power of their emotions? I no longer believe that was helpful. Even when I assisted people in uncovering long-buried emotions, I seldom encouraged them to savor the life-juice of the feelings themselves: the rich dark love-nature of grief, the warming fire of anger, the subtle luminosity of loneliness, the pure gut-driving power of sexual desire, or the exquisite clarity of fear.

Instead, for the most part, I helped them cope. I have come to hate that word, because to cope with something you have to separate yourself from it. You make it your antagonist, your enemy. Like management, coping is a taming word, sometimes even a warfare word. Wild, untamed emotions are full of life-spirit, vibrant with the energy of being. They don't have to be acted out, but neither do they need to be tamed. They are part of our inner wilderness; they can be just what they are. God save me from coping. God help me join, not separate. Help me be with and in, not apart from. Show me the way to savoring, not controlling. Dear God, hear my prayer: make me forever copeless.

COLD

A couple of years later I received another teaching, one that finally, I believe, made me get the point about fear and the folly of trying to control nature. It was February, the first time I had gone to the mountain in winter. I had been out alone many times by then, but never in the winter. I had very little cold-weather gear and no experience, so the weekend before I left, I set up my tent in the snow of my backyard for practice. I waited until late in the day so as not to be conspicuous, but still my neighbor walked over through the snow.

"What ya doin'?"

"I'm going camping next weekend and I've never been out in this kind of weather before, so I figure I need a little practice." I smiled. I had pretty much rehearsed it.

"Um. Gonna sleep out here tonight?" Blank face.

"Yeah," I smiled again.

"Well, hope you don't freeze." A smile back, finally.

I learned a lot that night. I learned how important it is to stay dry, to keep snow out of the tent and wear only enough clothing to keep warm. Sweat is no friend in cold weather; it stays on you and freezes. Equipment works differently too: the freshest flashlight batteries seem half used up, matches don't want to light, plastic becomes brittle. My family had given me a tiny single-burner gas stove for Christmas. In the cold it had to be preheated before it would start. I learned how to do that, and I made a cup of tea in the snow in the backyard. The water took a long time to boil.

I didn't have a cold-weather sleeping bag, just a couple of old thin ones, so I put one of them inside the other. It was an exhausting operation to get inside them, to zip them up, and finally to find comfort while hardly being able to move. I learned to take care of absolutely everything before I crawled into the bags; it's not a procedure to keep repeating. Once I was in and settled, my feet were freezing. How could my toes be aching from cold when I was inside two sleeping bags, fully dressed and wearing long underwear and three pairs of socks? Somehow I sensed my toes were not only cold but numb; the extra socks were too tight, cutting off the circulation.

Like Houdini in a straitjacket I managed to remove two of

the three pairs of socks without getting out of the sleeping bags, and warmth came. With a wool hat on my head, snuggled in, aware for the first time that snowflakes do make little sounds, I finally slept. Some hours later, I learned another lesson. Having to extricate myself from the sleeping bags, I resolved never again to drink tea just before going to bed.

The following weekend as I packed the car I felt calm, sufficiently prepared. No lists. Instead, I just moved slowly, trying to be open to what I might need. The only conscious plan I had—and I have no idea where it came from—was to cook a monster breakfast the first morning, a breakfast that might well last the whole weekend, a breakfast unforgettable, a breakfast that would move galaxies by its very existence. On my way I stopped at the grocery store and bought a dozen eggs, a pound of sausage and corresponding quantities of potatoes, onions, green peppers, mushrooms, cheese, and bread.

As I drove into the mountains, the sky was overcast and sleet was falling. An ice storm had struck the forest the night before and hundreds of trees lay broken by the wind force and ice weight. Here and there sunlight found its way through the gray clouds and everything glistened. The roadways to the campsite were slick and dangerous and the ranger had given me an alternative route, a longer one he thought might be a little safer along the mountainside. I was in four-wheel drive the whole time but I still skidded, slid, and spun my wheels.

I had to get out and pull two heavy broken branches off the trail into the site, and the only place I could park was up against some ice-bent bushes and low trees that scraped the side of the car. I had been so focused on the driving, so intent on staying on the road, that I missed the precious sense of welcoming I had come to love so much. I felt a little sad when I finally stepped out into the snow, realizing that all the way through the forest I had been coping with the ice, pitting myself against it, tightly controlling the car upon it. As dangerous as the ice was, I could not bear to begin my weekend with such a sense of antagonism, such single-minded lack of appreciation for my surroundings.

It was still early, the wind easing into fitful breezes, the sun shining more steadily, the ice-glazed forest bursting with radiance where the light touched it. I felt the familiar relaxation of my shoulders, my breath gentling like the breeze. Slowly I got back into the car. Without really thinking the thoughts, I was going to drive those icy roads just a little more, drive them this time with friendliness and simple respect, move along them as sweetly as I possibly could. I backed the car out of the campsite and drove perhaps a mile along the mountainside, then turned around and came back.

I drove with great attention, but now it was appreciation instead of antipathy. I drove carefully, but with a sense of participation rather than control. I felt vitally present, but there was no tension in me. And instead of concentrating exclusively on the driving, my awareness was open. I sensed not only the turns and slants of the road and the traction of the wheels on the ice, but also the forest around me and the sky above, the misty coldness of the air, the crystalline perfection of trees both fallen and still standing, the simple centered presence of my body, the way my hands held the steering wheel almost ten-

derly. Trees still whole after the storm softly shone in ice coat-
ing. The broken edges of fallen trees radiated sparkles, their
fractures fracturing the light.

I returned to the campsite in a completely different frame
of mind. As I again maneuvered the car up against the icy bush
branches, I felt ready to accept the Power of the Slowing whenever She chose to come. And She was right there, seeming to
guide me in walking on the icy snow in the same centered, open
way I had driven the car, moving with my center of gravity always
over my feet, never letting my feet or my head move much forward
of my belly, like a dance, a soft, confident choreography fully
open, conscious, present, and part of everything around me.

I set up camp gradually, smoothly, with no wasted motion. I
put my tent about ten feet from the car, near a stream that continued to flow through the cold, icing itself into steadily narrowing
channels, birthing fresh waterfalls over its own frozen substance.
The sky was overcast again and I could not see the sun setting.
The winter darkness came suddenly.

I tried to start a fire, but all the available wood was covered
with ice. Only fresh clusters of fallen pine branches, broken from
their mother trees by ice and wind, would catch the flames. The
frozen pitch within them melted, sizzled, caught and flared, and
then was gone. It was not the kind of fire that could give comfort
or cook a meal; it only offered sputtering hints of warmth. I was
not hungry anyway, and I knew I was going to have a monster
breakfast in the morning. The forecast was for clearing skies and
temperatures below ten degrees, so in the darkness I prepared to
preserve my body warmth in the tent.

In layers of clothing now wisely loose-fitting, a wool hat on my head and an insulating mat under me, I crawled into my doubled sleeping bag. The old zippers on the bags resisted, catching on folds of cloth, jamming as my numbing fingers tried to work them, but finally I was in and warm enough and I lay in the complete dark of a still-early evening, full of energy and not at all sleepy, with nothing to do.

SOUNDS

I am lying on my back, eyes open in the cold, seeing nothing. I hear the stream clopping and slapping against its icy walls, and chips of ice falling from trees when a spurt of night breeze bends them. But there is nothing else. Thoughts come and go, but I cannot follow them. The Power of the Slowing always stills my capacity to track thoughts to a conclusion. They simply appear, hover for a while like butterflies, then disappear.

One of the thoughts hazily drifting through my awareness now is that I'm not afraid. No crazy person, no bear, nothing in its right mind would move about on a night like this. I am all alone. Water and ice sounds. No fear. Faces come, images, people I know, people I don't know. I don't think about them, can't. Is this a prayer now arising? My mind tries to take it and make it something: my image of me praying, but I'm stilled again. If it's prayer, it just is. Prayer may be happening, but there is nothing for me to do. Images of home, of friends, of memories, things from the past come, and I sense them, experience them right now, here and now. I am warm inside. I wish I could stretch, move around, but warm is good.

Still not sleepy, just lying here. Am I bored? I don't know the difference between being bored and just being, and I can't even wonder about it much. I smile. My mind still wants to figure things out, still feels it has to be up to something, but it just can't do it. *Settle down, mind. My sweet, good-working, diligent mind, rest a while. It's okay, really.* The stream sounds are very loud now, suddenly a cacophony. I wish I'd camped farther away. *Settle down, little stream, you're deafening me. Settle down, mind.* Mind stream, building ice thoughts, flowing relentlessly, the nature of water, the nature of mind.

Sleep finally comes. Dream images no different from wakeful ones, stream sounds in the background, people talking, I'm really dreaming now. People talking, or are they playing a radio? Men and women talking, real voices. I wake, startled, tense, listening—Yes! They are voices, talking, God who's out here in this cold night? What are they up to? Straitjacketed in the sleeping bags I am tense as a twisted rope, so alert. They are voices for sure, talking to one another, yet I can't make out a single word. *What is this? My God, what's happening—am I nuts?* I focus in, hone my hearing right tight on the voice sounds. *What are they?* Now I know they're in the stream sounds. Voice sounds in the stream. Women and men talking, calmly, businesslike in the stream. My fear eases; I realize I've been holding my breath, straining to hear. As I relax, the voices are not so clear. They fade in and out of the stream sounds.

Something tells me this is a hallucination, and something else tells me it is absolutely real. My mind, to make something of it, wonders if these are spirit voices of ancient ones who died along these waters long ago. I hone my attention on them again, very directly, and I hear distinct words that seem to be made of English vowels and consonants, but not words I've ever heard before. Do I sense a little irritation in them now, as if they resent my eavesdropping? Oh, come on, Jerry. But it seems so real. I relax again, breathe, and the voices merge with water dropping, spilling, burbling on rocks and ice.

As sleep comes again, the voices wax and wane in tides and eddies and half-dreaming. I seem to see the faces of those who talk in the water, faces I've never seen before, but normal faces, women and men just talking, conversing calmly in the icy night in words I am not meant to understand. A time of stillness, of depth of sleep, and then another set of sounds. Once again I awaken, every sense sharper than I had ever thought possible. This time I am clear awake, no dazing fantasies possible, and someone or something is moving outside. I hear the crunch of footfalls breaking through the snow crust. I hear, right now, a scraping of those icy bushes over there against the side of my car—whatever it is, it's moving next to the car, up one side, down the other. I can see the bushes in my memory. They grow high, touching the sides of the car up along the windows. This must be something tall. This has to be a person.

I have never been so terrified, not in Vietnam, not anywhere. I thought I was helpless when the bear came, but it was nothing like this. I am lying completely vulnerable, unable to extricate myself from this prison of double-zipped sleeping bags. My fingers twitch feebly at my sides. There is nowhere to go, nothing to do, nothing to see, nothing even to smell, only hear the sounds and wait and be afraid, be fear.

Stretching with all senses toward the place of the sounds, I am amazed to hear whispered words coming from my own mouth. "Thank you, God. Oh, God, I thank you." Now, a fraction of a second after the whispered words, I am flooded by an immense feeling of gratitude. I am filled with it. I begin to move, slowly turning onto my stomach in the mass of fabric, not caring about the sounds my movements make, my knees drawing up beneath me, the sleeping bag tight against my back, my forearms on the ground. I could get out from this position. No need to unzip the bags. I could leap out if I needed to . . . for what? Why, for sheer gratitude!

The thankfulness feeling is overwhelming, so strong I cannot tell it from love. What is this? Terror-life-thanksgiving-love-power. My heart is thrashing from fear inside my chest, breath full, deep, clean, senses pure, vital. Do I really feel what this seems to be: my blood flowing in every artery, vein, and capillary, and each cell of me shining with life? And, oh, this mind, this awareness. Nothing inside but the clear radiance of living. God, I am so grateful, so overcome with thanksgiving for sheer being. Oh wonderful beauty love fear living being. *Thank you, thank you, oh thank you. I could die now, for I know what life is.*

No longer am I listening for outside sounds. I am only sensing my own terror-existence, the indescribable beauty, the giftedness, the sheer privilege. Oh my divine love, never again reassure me. I do not want to know everything will be all right. I never want to be secure again as long as I live. Give me no safety. Only give me this livingness forever, this power-of-being, though I know I will die of it, of love exploding.

The feeling passes. No sound remains but the stream and my heart. My hand pats around the tent and finds the flashlight. I unzip the flap and shine the cold-dulled beam toward the car, around the humble frozen fire ashes, over the stream. Nothing. I know now, dimly like the flashlight's beam, that although what makes me afraid might be deadly, the fear itself is wonderful. Fear is life-energy: full-bodied, rich, clean, exquisite, sweet. When you get right down to its bones, fear is love. Fear is *made of* love. That's why perfect love—love in its purest form—casts out fear.

I switch the flashlight off and roll over on my back, halfway out of the sleeping bags, my head sticking out of the tent flap, wool cap on the crusted snow, and there, once again, are the stars.

The stars must have knocked me out, for now it is morning and I am awakening, gently, back in the tent, snugly warm in the sleeping bags, unable to remember how I got here. The outer fabric of my sleeping bag and the whole inside of the tent are covered with a thin layer of ice, condensation from my breath. My life-breath has frozen itself all around me as I slept.

I crawl outside quickly and stand and stretch in crystalline air, the sky sheer blue, empty of clouds like my morning mind, empty of everything. I immediately walk to the car and look for tracks, but there are too many, most of them mine I'm sure, and I cannot tell one from another. I have no idea who or what made the footfall sounds in the night. So be it.

Kneeling by the fire pit, my mind in perfect morning empti-ness, I shake the brittle ice from the pine branches I tried to light last night. They light quickly and burn well now, and I inhale their sweet aroma. I boil water, make coffee, and with the mug in my hand and the third or fourth swallow in my stomach, my mind finally wakes up. *It's time for breakfast. The monster breakfast.* Ah, yes, my single plan, my one agenda. Like a slave to my thoughts, my body gets up to collect what I need for breakfast. I set my coffee mug on a stone near the fire and take one step toward the car and I am suddenly overcome with fatigue and the Slowing Presence arises wordlessly inside me, in a place much deeper than my mind, and it is telling me No, it is *not* yet time for breakfast, not at all.

I almost-feel gentle hands taking me by the shoulders, setting me back down by the fire. My body relaxes, my mind quiets. I sit. I look at the fire. I look at the morning mountainside. I close my eyes. There is no sound but the stream and the pine sap popping in flames. I watch the fire and I know time passes. Much time. Now and then thoughts of breakfast arise briefly and are stilled by the deeper sense, "Not now. Not yet." I just sit.

GUIDANCE AND TEACHING

It is difficult to describe the deep sense of guidance I experienced at times like that. I give words to it: yes, no, this, not that, now, not yet. But it doesn't come in words, nor even in thoughts. It's more like a kind of energy in a certain direction when the time is right for something, and a fatigue in that direction when it's not. Nature guided me, I think, by energy and lack of energy. Even now, years later, it continues, less dramatic but still extraordinary.

I still believe this is the most ordinary way of living, the natural way, the way of life for which we all are born.

Whatever the deep guidance is, it frees me from bondage to mind-thoughts. It liberates me from agendas, strategies, conditionings, and preconceived images. When that Nature-Power is strong, I no longer have to follow my mind away from the present moment into the abstract unconnected territories it wants to construct. Instead, I sense my thoughts and emotions in the same way I appreciate sights, sounds, smells, tastes, and touch: all cleanly, right here, right now, just part of what's going on.

What's going on is not just guidance, but also teaching. I am not meant to be a puppet, mindlessly turned this way and that by a Power not myself. The Power, as I called it then, is Wisdom, and Wisdom wants *me* to be wise, able to participate freely and fully in the dance of creation. So Wisdom guides me into situations and through circumstances where I learn the ways and the wonder of inner and outer Nature. Wisdom teaches Wisdom.

Thus I learned about fear. The basic lesson is this: Fear is not an enemy but a friend. Fear is something good, something alive, alert, and wild in us. Fear may be a response to danger, but fear itself is not dangerous. On the contrary, it is nothing other than life-spirit standing on its toes right here, right now with clear attention, sharp senses, ready body, flared nostrils, bristled hair, poised muscles, pumping heart, clean breath.

The immense gratitude I experienced when I was most afraid was for feeling so incredibly alive. In untamed fear there is a profound sense of something that is *me* going through the experience. It is personhood without definition, identity without identification, selfhood without attributes. And it has an immense steadiness to it, an almost eternal quality. Here is this life, this being that is deeply myself, having this experience, being in it as I have been through every moment of the past, as I will be in every moment to come, no matter what. In this strange way, fear brought me an ultimate reassurance.

I understand how people can become addicted to fear. I have known some who were hooked on their own adrenaline, compelled toward danger, driven to dancing with death at the edges of life. I doubt that will ever happen to me, for I have no desire to seek fear. But neither am I interested in protecting myself from it. When fear does come, I no longer want to cope with it. Let me neither tighten myself against what I'm feeling, nor become paralyzed by it, but let me live into the bright, sane responsiveness that fear makes possible. Let me welcome fear for the friend it is, for what it teaches and how it serves. When I feel the hairs on the back of my neck bristling for no reason, when I sense an unexplainable tremulousness, I never again want to deny it or call it neurotic. Instead, I want to welcome it, go into it, see what it is trying to show me.

People who have been assaulted sometimes say they had a premonition of danger but dismissed it. They judged their fear as unrealistic, denied or coped with it, and forged ahead. They were afraid of being afraid, and they got hurt. I have to disagree with Franklin Roosevelt and so many others who have said that the only thing we have to fear is fear itself. I would turn the phrase on its head and maintain that the only thing we have to fear is our fear of fear.[2]

BREAKFAST

It was at least two hours, more likely three, that I sat by the fire, and every time I'd think of breakfast I'd have the same fatigue feeling, "No, not yet." I sat there until my coffee was finished, and then I just sat there. I looked up and down the wintry hillside, at the ice-broken trees, at shadows and leaf piles that took on the appearance of frozen people. I stared at tiny crevasses in faraway rocks and thought I saw them move. I listened to the stream, and there were no voices in the daylight. I gazed into the glowing fire. I smelled pine sap in the smoke.

Perhaps I slept. I know I had long been still, body and mind unmoving, very slowed in breathing, when something seemed to move within me and I felt-heard, "Now. Now it's time." I was full of energy as I stood up and took a deep breath and looked at the sky and saw from the winter sun that it was well past noon. I piled more wood on the fire and set out the makings for breakfast.

My movements were unhurried, deliberate, appreciative. Next to the fire I placed a griddle for the sausage and vegetables, a frying pan for the eggs, and a pot of water for more hot coffee. Green peppers sliced, onions diced, white velvet mushrooms chopped, butter on the griddle steaming. Open my can of sliced white Irish potatoes, drain them, make a place for them on the griddle, add a little butter. Sizzle of the vegetables being seared, onion aroma blending with pine sap smoke, salt and pepper, *God, it's good to be alive.*

When the vegetables were simmering well, I pushed them to

the side and dumped a whole package of sausage on the griddle, broke half a dozen eggs into the frying pan and cooked them very, very slowly. Bread toasting-burning on the rocks, two slices of cheese waiting. A little catsup on the side for the potatoes. It was ready.

As I stood to get my plate I looked down at the thing I had wrought. There before me was the Queen Mother of all breakfasts. It was more huge, more beautiful than any description or even fantasy could portray. My single plan had been fulfilled beyond all dreaming. I went to the car and took out my camera and snapped four photographs of the breakfast, one from each point of the compass.

Then I sat and ate. I ate everything. Somewhere toward the end, well into the afternoon, I put down my coffee and opened a beer. That night, snuggled in my double sleeping bags, I slept the whole night through. No stream voices or snow crunches, not even any dreams that I recall.

I did not eat again the whole time I was there.[3]

Four

CICADA SONG

. . . the tranquil night at the time of the rising dawn,
silent music, sounding solitude . . .
—SAINT JOHN OF THE CROSS, *SPIRITUAL CANTICLE*

This is one of those stories that is likely to sound like a tall tale, and I can't assure you of the validity of my perceptions. All I can do is report what it was like for me. It happened on that very first trip to the mountain, on the second day, the day after the night of the bear. The night had been a teaching in the wisdom of here-and-now aliveness, an exercise of attention. My fears, the bear's visit, the cold hardness of the ground without a sleeping bag, the dreams that came—all these brought me to a clean, clear immediacy of Presence. And that immediacy prepared me to be bowled over by the glory of the stars, a beauty so powerful in the mountain midnight that it took my breath and my heartbeat and held them until I was almost sure I would die before it gave them back to me. Oh beauty of aliveness in the night!

AFTERNOON

I have the sense that more is to come. Last night was slim on sleep, to say the least. I awakened with the sunrise and I have been gritty-eyed and almost stumbling all day, everything in me slowed by fatigue. Now I am in the deep dull downtime, the afternoon valley, the slough that adrenaline leaves behind when it disappears like a withdrawing glacier. I lie here on my blanket beneath a tree, warm and easeful and longing for sleep, but I cannot sleep. The cicadas are too loud.

Their droning rises and falls, comes and goes in my ears and penetrates my bones. Occasionally I doze just a little into it, but then it becomes so loud or stops so suddenly that I reawaken. I am short of temper and fully irritated with the cicadas; they are interfering with my plans. Even in my dullness, my mind has been making plans—to take a nap and awaken fresh in the evening air so I will have the vigor to build another wonderful fire and cook a great supper and sing a welcome to the coming night. But everything seems to depend on this nap I must take now, this sleep I hunger for, and the cicadas are interfering with my plans.

It occurs to me, in the raspy kind of thinking that happens whenever I can't sleep, that every irritation in my whole life has come from something or someone interfering with my plans. There's a message here: have no plans and you'll have no problems. I hate the message. This afternoon I hate all messages. I am in no mood to be taught. I want only one thing now, and that is for the singing tree bugs to shut up.

"Quiet!" I shout, "Give me a break!"

They pay no attention. Crickets, frogs, birds, any sensible animal will go quiet at least for a while if you yell at it, but these cicadas either don't hear or don't care. I am quite certain they don't care. They live, it seems, in cicada world, the world of the present moment. I remember learning that cicada larvae spend from two to seventeen years under the earth sucking root juices in the silent darkness until one single summer when they rise into the light and molt, sing and court, mate and die. This year there is a huge crop of them, each one getting all it can out of its brief blessed time in the sun. They must have begun their singing around midday, but I failed to notice them.[4]

I see now that what cicadas do is mess with your consciousness. They start singing so gradually that you don't quite hear them until they're really underway, and then they keep going so steadily you tune them out. Then they suddenly stop and you sense the quiet and wonder where it came from. Then, just as you're getting used to the silence they strike up again and you're right there with them for a while, until they become a drone, and you tune them out again, and that's when they stop. It could be a kind of calling, I guess, an invitation to this here-now moment, but what I want here and now is sleep and they don't care. So I just lie on my blanket in the heat, almost dozing in some moments, almost awakening in others. Perhaps I join the cicadas in a few truly present moments. But I do not sleep.

Dusk comes, and hunger. I must have rested, for I find a fresh energy coming with twilight. Within the reverberations of cicada song I gather wood slowly, attentively. My movements feel graceful as I form the fire bed and light it. With the flames licking large in the evening breeze and coffee brewing there, I cook my supper: a can of baked beans bubbling in the coals, bread slightly burnt upon the flames, a can of beer. Not much of a feast, but I am very much into the heaven of it, and the cicadas sing and sing. Now I am hearing them all the time. I no longer tune them out. I am no longer dulled or lulled, and through no effort of my own I hear and see and smell and taste and feel everything.

Cleaning up after supper involves rinsing my fork and dropping the bean and beer cans into a plastic bag. In the very last twilight I get my drum out of the car. Yes, I admit it; I brought my drum. I'm not sure why; it wasn't on my list.

Now, as my hands touch the drum's rough wood sides and rawhide skins, I know it was part of my subliminal plans for my first wilderness solitude: something native, primal, aboriginal. I remember the Native American woman who sold it to me months before. She said traditionally only men played such a drum, and I should beat it with a stick, never with my hands. She said the drumbeat was the heartbeat of the earth. Now I am sitting cross-legged by the fire with this gentle drum on my lap and my right hand holding the leathered drumstick, poised. I feel totally silly.

It is difficult to be embarrassed all alone in the middle of nowhere, but I have accomplished it. Here I am, a middle-aged, middle-class white man from the suburbs sitting by a fire all alone in the mountains with a drum on my lap. I have no context for it, no tradition, no meaning. Perhaps one of my ancient ancestors once sat by a fire and beat a drum, but there is no memory in my family of such a thing, no memory in me. Is this drum supposed to symbolize something for me? Could it *be* the heartbeat of the earth? I think not.

I glance into the darkness, expecting someone there, the long-dead ghost of some true aboriginal, pointing at me and laughing. I feel my face warming. It could be the fire-heat, but I'm pretty sure I'm blushing. If I beat this drum now, who will hear? A skunk or two, a rabbit, perhaps a family of possums, the bear who came last night? I know the cicadas won't care. What will any of them care? I strike the drum.

It utters a dull thump, no resonance, no reverberation, the sound dead immediately, muffled in the trees, absorbed in cicada sound. I strike the drum twice more, three more times and each beat is taken into the trees and into the song of the cicadas, digested there, and gone. I feel small and somehow empty here by the fire in the center of this great sphere of night. My drum sound seems hopelessly impotent, helplessly overwhelmed by the loudness of the cicadas and the heaviness of the trees. Again some vague plan of mine is defeated, yet I suddenly realize that I am again wholly and completely in the present moment. I stop, the drumstick poised in midair, and for the first time I *really listen* to the cicadas.

They sing now in the night just as they have sung through the afternoon and evening. A thousand times they have called me to the present moment, and yet I have not until now truly listened to them, not directly, not with my ears perked toward them. I sit without moving for a long time, hearing them head-on, more attentive than I have been at any time since the bear last night. I am learning something about the cicadas this way; some mystery is disclosing itself. In the great undulating drone of their song I discern the sounds of individual cicadas, each contributing its own pitch and resonance. It is not just one sound but a vast composite, a texture woven of multiple buzzings, and the rise and fall of the sound comes from the simple number of insects who buzz, each in its own way part of the whole.

I notice that the drone is not a steady sound at all. It reveals an underlying rhythm, and the rhythm also is a composite, an intricate summation of cadences. One cicada's rhythm joins that of another to generate a third conjoint beat, so that two insects create at least three rhythms. My mind fails as I try to multiply that by the number of bugs in the trees. But I realize now there are far fewer cicadas there than I would have thought. Not thousands, not even hundreds, maybe only a score or two.

Sensing the rhythms within the drone, I begin to beat the drum with them. I try to pick out a cadence and follow it, but it feels too complex; I cannot tell one pulsation from another for more than a few moments. Then, in the way I have learned to receive gifts, I quit trying. Relaxing, I just beat the drum, allowing my own rhythm to emerge and find its place in the overall sound. Then a wonder: I sense a change in the cicada song, a subtle shift that seems to be a response to my joining them. It is the first and only time I have sensed cicadas responding in any way to my presence. It is completely dispassionate and yet strangely welcoming, as if each insect in its buzzing has adjusted itself a tiny bit to create a space for me, for my sound.

I am lost now, lost into the firelight's flickering on the tree leaves, warmth mingling with cool night star sparkles, all into the cicada song; I have been shown the way into the joining. I have been guided in a harmony path, to a oneness within which I am, once again, freshly and absolutely alive.

UNIVERSE SOUND

As I describe the experience now, it seems profoundly mystical. Yet I cannot adequately express how ordinary it felt, like the simple act of taking a breath and relaxing, entering this real here-and-now moment, letting things be exactly what they are, joining the plain truth of what simply is. There was even a part of me that kept watching from an almost scientific vantage point, a mindfulness that observed the happenings with gentle curiosity. I noticed, for example, that the cicadas I had heard all day resided in just two trees, one about six feet southeast of my tent, the other perhaps fifteen feet southwest, directly south of my fire.

The trees were about twenty feet apart, and I further noticed that instead of all the cicadas singing at once, the communities within each of the trees were alternating. First the group in one tree would sing, and as their sound waned the group in the other tree would begin. There was no doubt in my mind that the two communities were singing in response to each other. It was only after my drumming had joined the sound of the tree closest to the fire that I sensed this responsive way of singing. The rhythm of my drumbeat, which had so gently joined with the group of cicadas in the closest tree, was answering the group in the other tree, becoming softer as their sound rose, growing as theirs ebbed. Yet it was also, all together, one sound.

An ancient Hindu tradition says that if you could go far enough out in space and still hear all the sounds of the earth, they would be joined together in one great resonance: the holy sound of Om. At any given moment all the buzzing of cicadas, all the jabbering of monkeys, the talking and whispering, laughter, sobs, and screams of people, the rustling of leaves, the crash of surf, all the rush of traffic and clanging of factories, all the sounds of singing and groaning, of birds and raindrops, of volcanic eruptions and falling snowflakes combine their diversities into one unity of intonation, the song of the life of the cosmos. I used to think this image was just a symbol. Now I believe it is the truth.

I do not remember how the drumming of that evening ended. I know I was very sleepy; the fatigue from the night before had caught up with me. The cicadas were still singing when I went to bed. I remember wondering if they would sing all night, and if I would be able to sleep in their sound. But there was no irritation left in my body; all my frustration was gone, dissolved in the experience of unity. I had for a while been a part of their song, and it seemed impossible for it ever again to irritate me. If I slept, I slept. If I lay awake, I would just listen to their singing. Present moment, complete. They had given me that.

Lying in the tent with one cicada tree to the southeast and the other to the southwest, I was even more aware of the two groups responding to each other. I shifted my position so that I lay on my back with my head to the south. The sound of one group clearly came to my right ear, the other to my left, cicada stereo. I was sound-cradled, gently rocked back and forth by their singing. I may have slept, but I remember their song continuing steadily for a long, long time. Somewhere in the middle of the night I became aware that the sound was softening. I listened more carefully and realized that very gradually, with each response, one or two cicadas stopped singing. Somehow I knew it was related to the temperature, the slowly deepening coolness of night stilling the voice of one cicada, then another. Each response was almost imperceptibly quieter than the last.

I rolled onto my stomach and lay very still, completely charmed by the subtle decrescendo, the most gradual drifting away of any sound I have ever heard. Before long only a few bugs were singing, and then, finally, only one in each tree. It was well into the night and I was both tired and entranced, but I am as certain as I can be that what I perceived next really happened. The two still-singing cicadas slowly moved down their respective tree trunks to the ground. At first their sound had come from quite high above me; now it was at ground level, the level of my ears.

It took them perhaps ten minutes to reach the ground, and then they began to move across the ground, crawling toward each other. As they drew closer together, the responsiveness of their songs blended more and more quickly until one would begin before the other was finished, and their sound was more harmony than response. Finally they met each other between the trees.

They sang as one for a few moments and then were still. The night was utterly silent, and I went to sleep in wonder.

I have had many strange experiences lying alone in my tent at night, some of which I'm sure must have been hallucinations or dreams. But this meeting of the two final cicadas was an actual event. In my mind the next morning I figured it must have had something to do with cicada romance, some kind of elaborate courtship, perhaps a mating ritual that protects against cicada inbreeding, an instinctive mixing of the gene pool with the tribe of another tree. But later I learned that only the males sing; only males have the tiny membranes on their abdomens with which to make their sound. So I have no idea what they were doing, those two emissaries meeting between their respective trees. It is just fine that I do not know what their cicada-purpose was. It is enough to know what they did for me that night. They showed me the joining, and brought me as deeply into the present moment as I have ever been.

WILD CONTEMPLATION

When the cicadas were interfering with my plans to take a nap, I felt they were manipulating my attention. They would wake me up to the present moment by suddenly beginning to sing. Then they'd drone on until my attention became dull and I tuned them out, at which point they'd stop singing and the very silence would reawaken me to the present moment. I didn't know it at the time, but they were giving me a postgraduate education in contemplation.

I have studied the psychology of contemplation for many years. I know contemplation is a state of awareness that is, among other things, wide-open and completely present to whatever is going on in the immediate moment. I also know that most of us aren't that wide-open or immediately present most of the time. Instead, our brains have learned to pay attention to specific tasks at hand by actively excluding background noises, distracting thoughts, and anything else that we deem irrelevant. The brain has to work hard to do this, which is why we become tired after long periods of concentration. But even when we aren't concentrating on anything in particular, our brains are still in the habit of tuning out steady background stimuli. That's what I had done with the cicadas. At first I was concentrating on getting some sleep, so I'd try to tune out the cicada song. They cooperated by droning steadily until my brain shut their sound out, but then they'd stop and the change would open my attention and bring it back to the present moment again.

It has always seemed to me that true natural presence, true wild being, involves no tuning out of anything. It must be absolutely contemplative—openly receptive to all the sights, sounds, smells, tastes, and feelings that exist in each immediate moment. I believe it is civilization, the taming of our nature, that has taught us to focus on a single task and tune out what we consider to be distractions. I acknowledge that we do have to do this to function well in our society—but it just isn't natural.

Nearly thirty years ago, neurological researchers found that adult domestic cats focus attention and tune out distractions much as adult human beings do. When a domestic cat is resting, it can tune things out quite completely. Sometimes, if a cat is sleeping comfortably in its favorite napping place, you can even pick it up without waking it. And when stalking a mouse, a cat becomes nearly oblivious to everything else; you'd almost have to set off a firecracker to get its attention. In matters of attention, then, cats are very much like people: dull when they're comfortable, tunnel visioned when they're intrigued by something. I used to think cats were very contemplative, but according to these studies they are not.[5]

I had long wondered about these observations because neither dullness nor focused attention is very wise unless you're in an absolutely secure situation. Both would be dangerous in the wild; any decent predator could half-swallow a comfortably sleeping cat before it woke up, or could easily sneak up on one that was single-mindedly stalking a mouse. It's clear, however, that wild cats are very different. African lions hunt in coordinated teams—when stalking, they need to be attentive not only to their prey and competing predators, but to their hunting mates as well. Mountain lions hunt alone, but in stalking they will often take a downwind side route, moving ahead of their prey to find a tree or rock from which to pounce in ambush. Such stalking requires a keen, open, unfocused awareness of landscape, scents, wind shifts, and a host of other perceptions all at once; it simply *must* be contemplative.

The focused stalking of domestic cats seems crude, almost

lazy compared to the open contemplative attentiveness of wild cats. It is the essence of the difference between domestic and wild, between tameness and freedom, between safety and danger. For me, it is the difference between going through the motions of life and really living. I know of no studies on the neurology of attention in wild animals—and I hope there will never be any, for brain implants are required to do it—but I imagine most wild animals neither tune out nor focus their attention very much. When I say they are contemplative I am not romanticizing them; they simply could not survive without open, clear awareness.

Domestic animals, in their protected houses, barns, and stalls, don't have to worry about sudden attacks by predators. Neither do they need to track and stalk to find food. A house cat can afford to have a focused, one-track mind about stalking; dinner will be served whether it catches the mouse or not. Even though cats look deadly serious when stalking, they are really playing, as human beings play, expressing only a fancy of their buried wildness.

I think all babies, animal and human alike, are naturally contemplative. We are born open, present, unfocused, here-and-now. In civilized human society, we teach children to focus their attention, to fend off distractions, to concentrate on the particular task in front of them. This may be necessary for learning in the ways our schools are conducted, but we should know that we are training our children out of their natural contemplative presence, teaching them to devalue it, even perhaps to fear it. Children with attention deficit disorders tend to be more naturally contemplative, but they can have tremendous difficulty in our focused civilization. We treat them with drugs.

When it comes to the training of young animals in the wild, things are very different. Whereas human teachers tell children to pay attention to one thing at a time, I am convinced mother mountain lions, wolves, and other predators teach their young the opposite: not to become too absorbed in any one thing, to keep their senses open. These animal teachers hone the natural contemplative awareness of their young. A mountain lion cub, like a young human child, easily becomes preoccupied with a plaything. At such times, it is especially vulnerable to attack. When it comes time for training, the mother mountain lion teaches her cubs to watch out for themselves, to remain open and sensitive to sights, sounds, and smells coming from any direction at any time. This is an essential part of their training, for hunting as well as self-protection.

Domestic animals and wild animals raised in captivity usually do not survive when released into the wild. They do not know how to hunt, and they are too trusting to protect themselves from predators. If such are the effects of domestication upon animals, what price do we human beings pay for our civilized awareness? By the time we reach adulthood, most of us are so conditioned to focusing attention that the concentrated one-track mind is the only way we have of approaching situations. As we mature, we may be vaguely aware of missing something, but we are too far away from it even to give it a name.

What we are missing is fullness of life. To put it simply, in concentrating on one thing at a time, we miss everything else. Going shopping, we miss the sky. Doing work, we miss the singing of birds. In conversation with one person, we ignore the presence of others. Through it all, we fail to appreciate our own precious *be-ing*—the soft flow of breath, the beating of heart, the subtle beauty and wisdom of body, the sheer pristine wonder of being aware. One could say these are only aesthetic qualities, unimportant in handling the real tasks of daily life, but our handicapped awareness has serious and far-reaching practical implications as well.

Like domesticated animals, we are completely unprepared for the wild—the wild outdoors, the wild in our cities, the wild in our own psyches. In any of these places, we panic when we're lost and afraid. We frantically concentrate our attention here and there, following nonexistent tracks, unaware of a thousand clues from sky and light and smell and inner Wisdom that could tell us where to go and what to do. Feeling so divorced from the nature within and around us, we make wildness an adversary that we must tame rather than join, master rather than learn from. Wherever we find it, we feel we must force Nature into the tunnel of our own concentrated vision. That's what brings us to manage natural resources, engineer social change, strategize our child-rearing and human relationships, control our emotions, and cope with our stresses.

There are, of course, places for focused awareness. I'm happy that my airline pilot and my surgeon are able to concentrate on their checklists and technical procedures, but I hope they have plenty of contemplative presence as well. When the checklist is complete, I hope my pilot will be open to all stimuli at once, the sound of the engines, the look of the surrounding sky, the feel of the controls, simply present to everything as a whole. And I hope my surgeon will pause frequently to take a breath and sense the subtleties that don't fit into lists and procedures, to be attentive not just to the rate of my pulse and breath but to their gentle rhythms as well, and to all the sights and sounds and smells and feelings and intuitions of each precious moment. In any activity, in any setting, it is this contemplative possibility that makes the difference between simple technical correctness and truly accurate responsiveness.

My hunch is that life needs 95 percent openness and 5 percent concentration, and we have the proportions reversed. I wish we could encourage our children's natural contemplative awareness as well as their capacity to concentrate. And I wish that we adults who have been trained-away from contemplative presence could have a teacher to show us where the present moment is. All it takes is Someone or Something to point us in the right direction, and then, when we look there, we discover teachers waiting everywhere: inside trees, animals, wind, and stars, in the pristine eyes of little children, and in our own souls.

The cicadas taught me many things on that first trip to the mountain. The most profound teaching—about joining and harmony and the welcoming space all things make for one another in fundamental oneness—is something I cannot express in words. But what they taught me of immediate awareness is very clear and precise. Cicadas can be messengers of immediacy for us all. In mountain forests or inner-city streets on a summer afternoon, the song is there for the listening, "Be here now, Be here now, Be here now." All it takes is ears to hear. The listening is everything.

Cicadas, of course, don't exist simply to remind forgetful human beings to wake up to the present moment. Like all creatures, like all people, cicadas are ends in themselves. Cicadas live in cicada time, in cicada cycles, in the world of their long darkness and their brief time to sing. But in the interconnectedness of everything, rays of cicada song, tendrils of cicada presence spin out to touch and enter the worlds around them, to interweave with the lives of other bugs, and of trees and earth and birds and human beings.

In pure immediacy it is finally impossible to distinguish who is touching whom, who is teaching whom, what is being taught. That evening by the fire, in that wordless spacious endless interconnection, I might even have taught the cicadas something about the deep essential goodness of human sounds, however clumsy they might be.[6]

Five

OF TIME
AND THE SEASONS

How do you endure
Oh life, not living where you live . . .
—SAINT JOHN OF THE CROSS, *SPIRITUAL CANTICLE*

The cicadas taught me about the present moment, which got me thinking about time. In our culture, we see time as a moving stream, beginning way back in the past somewhere, flowing forward through history to the present and on into the future. We can almost feel its movement, slow and plodding in our youth, passing quickly as we age, only rarely standing still. We apply linear measurements to the flow of time: minutes, hours, centuries, eons. These allow us a certain sense of security; we believe that all events happen in the orderly, reliable procession of the stream of time.

As our technology becomes more complex and our measurements more precise, time takes on an almost palpable quality. It seems substantial, objectively real, a thing to possess and use. It even becomes a commodity. Time is money, we say, and, like money, we never have enough of it; we want to spend time wisely, invest it profitably, save it wherever we can. Like money, time is not to be wasted, lest we run out of it. And like money, time drives us, obsesses us, enslaves us.

We easily admit that money is a medium of exchange, that it only represents the goods and services it can buy. But while money can be held, touched, and seen as well as counted, time permits only the counting. When we try to hold it, it is already gone. Physicists have been proving the insubstantiality of time for generations. Time is so interwoven with space, matter, and energy as to be finally indistinguishable as a thing in itself. Such observations interest us, but most of us don't spend much time reflecting on them. It would be a waste of time.

I have in my mind a conversation with a voice-equipped cicada. "You must know time very well," I tell him. "You spend years under the earth in darkness, then come out so briefly to the light. Tell me something about the nature of time. What is it, really?"

"Time?" I hear him ask me. "What is time?"

"That's what I want you to tell *me*. I'm talking about things like how long you stay underground, or how long you have in the trees, or maybe," I add with a male-bonding grin, "how long it takes you to, you know, mate."

"How long? What is 'how long'?"

"Well, 'how long' is about time—like how many times a second you vibrate your belly-drum when you sing, or how many seconds or minutes or hours your lovemaking lasts."

"Seconds? Minutes? Hours?"

"They're measurements of time."

"Ah, yes, time." He is beginning to sound like a Zen master.

I try again. "Think about years: winters, springs, summers, you must know these very well."

"Cooling, warming, stilling, moving, dark, light, yes?"

"Yes, that's it! That's what I want to know about."

But my mental cicada is now in full Zen master mode, and he seems to like it. "You tell me, Jerry, what is time?"

I have to stop the fantasy, for my imaginary cicada can take me no further than my own thoughts normally do, and thinking of time I keep coming around to emptiness. If I could, I would ask a real cicada about the present moment. But I know there would be no understanding, because even the present moment is a time measurement. It is the supposed point of now, mentally drawn on an imaginary line between our concepts of past and future.[7]

Nature, I think, knows nothing of concepts of time or of the present. Nature—our own and that of the world around us—lives in *Presence* instead of "in *the present*." Rather than moving through time, it simply exists in cycles and successions: sound and silence, light and darkness, birth and death, activity and stillness, courting and nesting, eating and sleeping. Everything is rhythms. Everything is seasons.

SPRING COMES EVERY YEAR

It was a very human Zen Master from Korea who planted the mystery of the seasons in me. It was the late 1970s, and we at the Shalem Institute had invited Seung Sahn Soen-sa Nim to be part of a conference of spiritual leaders at the National Cathedral. He was a small muffin of a man out of whom giggles erupted repeatedly like startled butterflies. He was a moonbeam of relief in the conference's heavy clouds of theology. When it was his turn to speak, he began with the old story of a Zen student who had a profound question to ask his Master. After looking in several places, the student finally found his Master cleaning out a latrine with a wooden stick. The student bowed and asked, "What is the Buddha, truly?" The Master immediately held up the stick and said, "Shit on a stick."

The point, as I understood it, is that absolute reality is exactly what's going on here and now, nothing more, nothing less. What was going on there and then as I heard the story was that I was sitting next to my son Paul. He was about ten at the time. I had brought him along thinking he might enjoy the Cathedral and learn something about the work I was doing, which has always been a mystery to my kids. Paul had done his best to remain awake and dignified during the conference, but it hadn't been easy. Even I had been a bit bored. But when the Zen Master began his story, Paul immediately sat up, attentive and smiling. And upon hearing the word *shit* spoken in those holy Gothic halls,

Paul nearly exploded. "*Shit*," Paul tried to whisper. "He said *shit* in church!"

Then, helplessly, Paul became a little Zen Master himself. He chortled and sputtered and hugged his stomach and turned all pink and rolled on his side in the pew until the laughter tumbled out of him and over all the people in the audience who were pondering the deeper meanings of the Buddha being shit on a stick. Paul's laughter caught them, caught us all and broke us open in a little satori moment and we all laughed and the Zen Master laughed the biggest laugh and then everyone laughed harder and it was nothing but delight.

In the social hour that followed, Paul went off exploring the cathedral, but he kept returning to me and whisper-giggling, "Shit on a stick. Shit on a stick." I signed a copy of my just-published first book for the Zen Master, inscribing it with something about my great respect and admiration for him. When I gave it to him, he wrote an inscription in Korean in one of his little Zen texts and offered it to me with a glance over in Paul's direction. "Shit on a stick," he said, and everyone started laughing again. I asked him to translate the inscription he had given me. Slowly pointing to each character, he read, "For Jerry: The tongue has no bone. Spring comes every year. Love, Me."

I bowed and smiled knowingly, though I didn't have a clue what the words meant. I had expected something like "For Jerry, with gratitude for your contributions to the integration of psychology and spirituality." But I got that there's no bone in the tongue and spring comes every year. Okay. I'd sit with it awhile.

OF KNOWING

It was nearly fifteen years before Nature began to show me the meaning. Of course the tongue has no bone and spring comes every year—that's the way things are. And that's the point: everything is just the way it is. Present moment or not, no matter what ideas and concepts we have, things are still just what they are. Nature always tells me this. I sit and gaze at a tree in the spring, new green buds just emerging, dark moist bark glistening in the sun. I think about new life, resurrection, hope. I might even give the tree a personality and a story: she stood steadfastly through the winter, patiently gestating her springtime possibilities, and now she begins her birthing. In a few weeks she will be pale green exuberance. But beneath my lovely thoughts, Nature invites me to really look at the tree and just see her for herself. As my gaze deepens, all commentary stops and there's just the being of the tree, the tree being tree, beyond even my label of "tree," and me being me with no self-images and it's all one complete immediate being-experience, breathlessly exquisite.

Sometimes my imagination can symbolize a tree beautifully, but it's still commentary. And commentary requires that I set myself apart from the tree, make an object of it in order to have thoughts and feelings *about* it. Even if my feelings are strong, even if I fall in love with it (which happens very easily with certain trees), I am still separate, me standing here adoring the tree there. What I feel is not tree-feeling but only my heart's response to it. Need I say that this is true with human relationships as well as with anything else in creation?

At times in my life I have tried to resign myself to an inevitable subject-object separation. But love keeps wanting to bridge the gap, to bring all separations together. Love and Nature—and I'm not sure there is a difference—show me that although separation may be a necessary part of the cycles of experience, it is not meant to be constant. The gift of joining, of direct, participative communion, is a very real possibility in every moment. When my comments cease and my symbols evaporate and my feelings dissolve into pure Presence, I join the tree in its real, immediate being. Then I "know" nothing about the tree or me or anything else. What I feel is not emotion but sheer perception: the touch of breeze on my skin, the pressure of ground on my feet, my heart's pulse, the needle entering my vein for chemotherapy, whatever is there. I have nothing to show for the experience, nothing to hold onto within it. But I am, for the moment at least, in the fullness of life. As the tree is, always.

This is the wilderness of being. It is what Wisdom showed me, where Nature has always taken me. It is Her home, Her dwelling, the place of Her abiding, the sacred household of being-as-it-is where all creation is at home in its wildness and nothing is domesticated. Sometimes I picture Wisdom standing in the doorway of Her being-home, sweetly calling me toward Herself. Or She might come up from behind and gently nudge me there. Sometimes She shows up inside me, and I find myself unknowingly urged in that direction, from within. And occasionally, perhaps impatient with my stumbling, She becomes a mother mountain lion, taking me by the neck in Her powerful mouth, carrying me home, setting me down exactly where I need to be.

I still have the Zen master's little book, and I hold it in my hands now, gazing at his inscription. I see traces of Her Presence here, in the twenty-seven characters he wrote with a felt-tipped pen on this now-yellowed page. Perhaps Wisdom moved his hand as he wrote, but I think it was far more intimate, more interwoven than that. No matter; it is Wisdom's message and his message, old ink, yellow page. The just-is-ness of life. No commentary. Shit on a stick. This book in my hands. These words in my mind. No bone in the tongue. Spring does come every year.

OF THE SEASONS

And so do summer, fall, and winter. My inner commentary about the seasons is very complex. It has to do with movements of earth and sun. At one level, which I can call "sense commentary," I directly see the sun rise in the morning, move across the sky, and set in the west in the evening. But at another level, my "thought commentary," I know it's not the sun moving; it's the earth.

My mind knows that seasons happen because of something we might call an imperfection—the earth's axis is tilted in relation to the sun. If everything were straight lines and right angles, the earth's equator would always be in line with the sun and we would have no seasons. Each day would be exactly the same, all year round. But straight lines and right angles seldom happen in nature.

So the sun does not rise and set exactly in the east and west. In summer, as the earth turns, the sun appears and disappears over the horizon somewhat toward the north, appearing to go higher in the sky, making longer days, warming things. In winter, its apparent path is more southward and lower; the days are shorter, the nights longer, everything colder.

The sun appears to change, but really it's the earth, turning on its tilted axis once a day and revolving around the sun once a year. That is how my thought commentary explains it. Outdoors, though, I could still swear it is the sun doing the moving. It clearly rises somewhere toward the east, glides slowly across the sky, and sets in the west. As the seasons change, I *see* the sunrises moving northward and southward along the eastern horizon, the sunsets doing the same in the west.

Sometimes, watching a sunrise, thoughts stop and senses have full reign. At other times my senses fade a little and I think about what I'm experiencing. Often another commentary happens, something more aesthetic: a sense of beauty, or of joy or reverence. I could call this a "feeling commentary," my interior emotional response to the experience.

There are probably many other commentaries besides thoughts, senses, and feelings, but I see no reason to enumerate them. Sometimes one commentary comes to the fore and suppresses the others. Sometimes they all swirl together in one inordinately wonderful experience of nonsensical sensing. Sometimes I don't care.

And occasionally, more and more often now, the commentaries stop altogether, and there I am, open to everything, making nothing of anything, and everything is just as it is. I am like I was as a baby. I feel the warmth of sunlight, the cold of night air, but no labels. I breathe, and it's simply breathing happening. Sometimes snow falls. Taste of snowflakes on my boneless tongue.

HORIZONS

To appreciate the seasons fully, you need a horizon. You need a completeness of sky, a place where your view of it can be *horizon-tal* as well as vertical. I have grown accustomed to horizons, and a part of me goes hungry when I've been too long without one. My house is surrounded by other buildings, so I often went to two nearby places that have wonderful horizons. One is the reservoir where I took my canoe. The other is an expanse of fields and meadows on gentle hills, about ten miles to the north. Now my body is too frail to handle a canoe, or even to walk the fields. But my memories of being there are sharp and clear.

In the place of fields and meadows there is a giant tree stand-ing nearly alone, with only a few saplings and vines in attendance. I don't know if the tree is female or male, or even if the species has gender, but to me she seems a matriarch, a great solitary Queen. I watch the tree first through winter: twisted dancing branches caught frozen against the gray sky, black lines, even more black dressed with snow, still and stark even when the wind growls and shifts. I walk eastward over a small hill in the February dawn and there she stands, hefty in trunk and wide at the top like a huge stalk of broccoli, more within the sky than against it, the dawn lightening behind her and she is a deep black dancing skeleton holding still while I am watching her. As I stand there, the sun's round yellow disk rises from the horizon a little to my right, south of the tree, and her black branches glisten.

In March I return, wanting to try to sketch her twisted

branches before her leaves come out. I am just in time, for already
she seems to wear a vague haze of greenness about her, a halo on
her outer edges so delicate that I am not certain it is really there.
I sit on the hill and sketch, striving to follow the intricate jagged
angles of her branches in the dawn. The sun rises again, this time
almost directly behind the tree's great trunk, and I have to move
an inch to the right so the light will not blind me and the tree
in silhouette is radiantly black against the cold sunrise fire. I can
draw for only a few more minutes before the sun burns round
her dark trunk and branches and her black is all radiance and my
eyes, even squinting, can no longer bear the brightness.

I come back three mornings in a row, just before sunrise, trying to complete the sketch. Each morning the lines seem different; she is the same and yet she has changed. I think I've caught
her; my sketch will be proof that she dances in the night when no
one is looking. Yes, her branches are not quite the same—I'm certain that one went up there and now, today, it's going off to the
left instead. But she is implacable, so still in the dawn that she'd
make you believe she's never moved in all her years, even that she's
winter-dead now, inanimate, but I know better. Each morning I
erase some lines, change them, add some new ones. I smile gently,
acknowledging my inability to keep up with her.

And each morning I must shift my position a few inches to
the right to protect my eyes from the sun that is rising a little
more northward each day. The sunrises are virtually galloping
northward now, and soon it will be the vernal equinox, the "equal
night" of springtime when the sun is halfway along its northward
journey on the horizon, halfway to summer. The tree, I am sure,

knows all about this, in perfect direct experience of tree-being through seasons too numerous to be counted.

When she was young perhaps her virgin leaves bent toward the sunrises, following them along the horizon, almost reaching, as my eyes now do. But now she is old, so heavily barked and deeply rooted and fully branched that she holds the earth and sky that hold her, and now she is simply greening because spring comes every year. In the far high distances of her, in the verdant aura around her outer edges, her newness is about to birth, and then there will be little sprouting leaf-petals that might turn in their own slight ways to follow the sun. But no one will ever notice their tiny turnings, not even I who watch her so closely. She is too huge, her greenness too high, too far away.

As the equinox passes, I see the sunrises "march" northward from the tree, more than a sun-disk's width each day. Over the next couple of months the northward movement of sunrises slows, slows until in late June it becomes imperceptible. This is the summer solstice—"sun standing still"—when the sun seems to cease its movement along the horizon, rising at its northernmost point and making its highest arc across the sky. It is the longest day and the shortest night of the year.

The tree is now lush in summer morning mist, exuberant in the warmth of afternoons. Through summer, the sunrises and sunsets move back toward the south each day, gradually picking up speed, "falling" south through the autumnal equinox. The tree's oval leaves turn crimson, a few at a time at first, then all rushing to keep up. Raucous vectors of geese fly, and the leaves fall. Chill comes. The tree's deep scarred bark seems to become

darker as the sunrises and sunsets slow in their southward movement. The sun's arc is lower, the days shorter, nights longer. Then
the place of sunrise stands still again at winter solstice and the
tree is once more a black skeleton, dead if you didn't know better.
Then, ever so slowly, the place of sunrise begins to move northward again.

JUST A LITTLE GRACE

On a winter evening I rest my back on the tree's great trunk and
watch the sun set far across a mounded white snow meadow, ruby
roundness settling steadily behind darkening tree-bones in the
distance, pink splashes through the western sky. For a long moment I am inside this particular sunset, rolling in it like a child
in new hay. I am simply experiencing; I must *be* the experience,
for it is all there is. Then self-awareness comes, recognizing the
beauty and the bliss, wanting to prolong it, somehow to hold it
forever, and I know I am here, having this experience. The self-
consciousness makes me feel just a little separate from the sky
and the soft bark of the tree on my back and the sun now gone
beyond the horizon. Now I am an observer, an experiencer, and
this sunset has become something I am perceiving, an experience
I'm having.

In an instant, thoughts come: memories of other sunsets, a
slight wishing for someone with whom to share the moment, a
little appreciation of God's goodness. The thoughts bring other
feelings: wonder, longing, thanksgiving, sadness, hope, praise.

Thoughts and feelings grow into interpretations, and interpretations into commentaries. I reflect upon the symbolism of sunsets. I even remember my astronomy and try to experience the sunset as the earth turning, the winter here because the tilted earth is revolving around the sun. And then, finally, my thoughts take me with them, toward what I have yet to do this evening, and tomorrow's busy schedule. It is late, I think, and time to go home. I walk away from the tree without looking back, as if she were not even there.

I was the experience, then the experiencer, then a commentator and interpreter and maybe even a bit of a controller, and finally I am gone, simply gone from the here and now, gone away from the tree and the last pink light in the sky. I do not hear the crunch of my feet upon the snow meadow, for in my mind I am already home, working on what needs doing for tomorrow.

It is easy for me to be judgmental about this sequence of consciousness, to say my first simple experience was so much more pure and pristine and fundamentally beautiful than the commentary that followed. But here's the thing: IT'S *ALL* EXPERIENCE! Every bit of it, the oneness and the separation, the immediacy and the distancing, it all happens when it happens, and when it happens it's as absolutely real as the snow and the tree and the sky.

With just a little bit of grace, I can *be* here, really exist here, present, open, available, immediate. With just a little grace I can see the sunset, feel the cold air, sense the beauty, feel my reactions, experience my thoughts arising and the emotions they engender, perceive my little attempts at control, experience my commentary, notice my leaving. And maybe, as my mind takes off somewhere on its own, I might even say good-bye to the tree.

It can all be an experience, within the present moment, with thoughts, images, senses, and feelings all embraced together, all unified in Being Now. I know it doesn't happen this way all the time, not even very much of the time. But the bare-naked possibility of it, the fact that life can be lived with such Presence is a wellspring of endless hope for me. And I want it. I yearn for it. I give myself to it because I have felt it and cannot shake the sense of its perfection. I stake my life on it because for me it is the place where you and I dance into realizing, *realizing* our eternal embrace of one another and the earth within God's endless, infinitely intimate embrace of everything. It is where the reign of heaven comes alive. It is soul freedom, love unfettered, and absolute compassion, all flowing from the tiniest gift of grace.

WISDOM AND WILLINGNESS

I don't know where or how the gift of grace might come. In those outdoor-wilderness years I called it the Power of the Slowing, the incarnate mercy of Absolute Nature moving into my willingness, opening my desire, deepening my relaxation, empowering my vulnerability, making me receptive to what is. It happens very rarely now, but Wisdom does still come to me that way sometimes, as if Her hands were touching my belly and massaging my shoulders and turning my head so I can really see and feel what is here and now, and know who I truly am.

I'm not sure, but our willingness for such an empowerment just might be everything. I think God respects our individual integrity and will not invade us when and where we are unwelcoming. But that is not to say we are ever left alone, no matter how we feel, because Wisdom keeps beckoning. From inside and outside, She does call. Moreover—and this I do not pretend to understand at all—She can, if we want it, empower our very welcoming, deepen our hospitality to Herself and Her world, ease our defenses and create within us a bottomless receptivity for Herself.

The first chapter of the Book of Proverbs says that Wisdom cries out in the streets and raises her voice in open places. It's true, I'm sure, because Wisdom is everywhere. The place of wilderness does not have to be outdoors; it could be anywhere. Finally, I suppose, it is always inside us. Wisdom lives for us wherever our wilderness is, in whatever is *Nature* for us—the place closest to our birth and birthing—and She calls us there and when we go there we find ourselves strangely welcomed and welcoming. And if we are willing for it—which I guess means simply relaxing into our wanting—She comes to show us what we need to know.

Beneath the sky and in the field or forest or on the water or even alone in my room, She will bring my attention to the horizon, and there to sun and earth and moon and all the sounds and presences of creation inside and out. There, in Her given moments, everything is what it is and I know I am a part of it and I can have any thought or feeling I want and it's absolutely fine because it's just part of Her day, and now, through God's grace, it's just part of mine.

So I don't have to make anything of it. Whatever is going on is sufficient. I don't have to work at it, nor do I have to restrain myself. I don't have to try to be assertive nor placid nor searching nor accepting. I don't have to try to do or be anything, but if trying is what I'm doing, that's fine too. I am free to be just who I am. Wisdom calls and leads me into my own nature, wordlessly encouraging me to be natural. If I *try* to be natural, She will whisper "No, no," in my ear and take me by the hand or, if need be, by the scruff of my neck, and show me, step-by-step, how to be myself without trying. When I get there, I see no trying was ever needed; it's not something to do, not even a way to be, but more like a place to be *in*, a place to stand, a place I go to that's really inside me all the time. It is home, my true home, the hearth of my spirit.

It is when I am in this abiding-place that everything comes together: experience and concept, beauty and truth, senses and thoughts, responses and comments, primal being and scientific knowledge. They all become one being, one experience, one appreciation, one sparkle in the radiance of being alive.

OF MISTS AND EMPTINESS: SPRING

At my other horizon-place, the reservoir, I remember slipping my canoe into the water of early springtime just before dawn. The water from the lingering night is warmer than the morning air and there are mists, eddying, rising, ever-moving water-clouds waiting to take me into them. I paddle with the softest, smoothest simplicity of which I am capable, wanting to dip into the stillness of the water and leave it undisturbed by sound or wave.

As I paddle into the mists they open for me and seem to retreat a little, making space, being respectful, but I breathe them in and if I hold very still I feel them exploring my skin. Among these gentle ghosts the canoe glides so flowingly that I could swear there must be space there, space between the canoe's smooth belly and the film of the water's surface tension, a thin space holding only mist and emptiness. And my scientific mind knows it is true; the canoe moves on mist and emptiness, just a molecule or two above the water, the water and the mist kindly making space in the not-yet-dawn of springtime morning.

The sun rises, lightening over the trees in not quite the place I expected, just as it did as I tried to draw the Matriarch tree. The mists seem almost busy now, brushing here, touching there before they have to return to air and water in the sunlight that is to come. In the dawning a slight greenness hovers around the black tree-shadows, a hint of plant-flesh on their bones. Color comes as the sun rises and the mists evaporate; bird sounds begin. In midspring the beginning of each day is a reenactment of the whole season's coming. The night has been like winter, blacks and grays and cold shadows. The dawn brings awakening, the slow birth of color and sound. Finally, the day is spring itself, the greening and the blossoms and the birds.

SUMMER

Canoeing in summer is a feast of delicious green, luscious humidity. The water under the sun becomes bath-warm and turns brown when it rains, and the canoe seems to ride lower in the water. Floating green-brown algae cling to the canoe just above the waterline. I want to see summer sunsets in my canoe. Evening is now more inviting than morning, for mornings are so much the same from one day to the next, so often already hot. Evenings bring more surprises; a wind might come, perhaps a storm. The sun both rises and sets in haze on many days, and sometimes the humidity is so high that the sun is just a blur, its light seeming to come from everywhere so that you don't even call it sunlight. It's just the day, the heat, the sweat you can feel smoothing the surface of your skin. Sweat has its own little surface tension and emptiness on your skin, and it becomes mist, it really does. The sun is very intimate in summer, no longer a celestial object but a being of great Presence and Power moving upon me, closing in. I can't follow it objectively because it seems to be everywhere, so close, part of my own body.

FALL

On an autumn morning in my canoe. The cool of the season is an arising freshness that can feel like new life even while the leaves are dying. Symbolically, fall is slow death, a retreat toward the underground tomb of winter. But in its immediate presence I feel the exquisite vulnerability of this season, a baring, a gentle disrobing into beauty down to the bones. We say the leaves are turning color, but they are actually revealing their true colors, their soft reds and oranges and yellows, the sun-colors that have been there all along, hidden by the chlorophyll of summer. The sun's southward travel and lowering in the sky, the briefening of days and cooling of air bring photosynthesis to an unhurried conclusion, the fading of green. So before they fall, the leaves disclose their beautiful nature-truth, more beautiful because it is more true.

Leaves have fallen on the water. They float upon the surface, on emptiness and hidden mist, and morning dewdrops—or perhaps the crystal remnants of forgotten splashes—glisten and christen their leaf-dryness in the clarity of dawn. I paddle to one yellow gem-carrying sycamore leaf and it slips away on its thin film of emptiness as the wood side of my canoe approaches. I lean gently, but the leaf drifts beyond my reach. As the canoe stills and then turns gently in the breeze, another leaf glides toward me bearing a single water droplet and I am allowed to lift the leaf and hold it toward the sunrise and clear rays sparkle from the droplet and sun is inside the droplet; the leaf bears the sun.

WINTER

The water company closes the reservoir to boating in December. Perhaps it is because of the danger of hypothermia as the water chills, or maybe it is simply and rightly to give the place a winter rest, to allow it stillness in the cold. Some Native Americans in the Southwest enter a phase of "keeping still" in this season, staying inside and quieting their activities just as animals and plants enter their own winter repose. Now the winter solstice approaches, when even the rising sun stands still on the horizon.

On the last permissible weekend I put the canoe into the pre-dawn water and skim slowly north. I pour instant coffee in the coldness, and the coming sunrise is ice fire in a sky of blue perfection. There is no wind; everything, the universe, is keeping still. The canoe moves tentatively on the quiet surface of the water as if it, too, is nearly ready to rest in its wintertime.

Ah, ice has formed there where the shallows are, prisms and feathery patterns in thinly frozen water. I paddle to it, gliding upon waters that are now strangely, deeply black in the clean absolute light. The ice is very thin here, exquisite, and the canoe's gentle bow-curve crinkles it crisply, and shards too slim to see on edge slide atop one another over the ebony water. They are frozen mist, fractured slices shimmering on the emptiness of surface tension. Does she know, my little canoe, that this is her last time out? Soon I am as surrounded by the ice as I was by the spring-time mists. This ice is not as respectful as the mist, less forgiving, now perhaps a quarter of an inch thick, etched in endless varieties of perfectly ordered line-patterns, a vast, intricate sketching in frozen water. It is divine geometry, including straight lines and right angles and everything in between, all formed with the infinite casualness of Nature. God is showing off again.

At the close of that last winter weekend my son Paul helped me carry the canoe into the basement and place her on sawhorses. By that time he was an English teacher, and now he's a writer. I wonder how vividly he remembers his little-boy hilarity about shit on a stick. During the next three months I will give many good hours to sanding and smoothing the canoe, working out her tiny ice scratches and her deeper scars from meetings with rocks.

My fingers will touch every part of her. I will learn how to work with epoxy resin. She has gone underground for the winter, as life in the wilderness does.

I will also take many walks then in the cold fields and in the meadows in the blessed snow, and I know that things are not dead then at all. Deer and rabbits quiet, fish and frogs and turtles nearly frozen, snakes holed up, summer birds gone away and winter birds now here, trees black and bare, seeds and cocoons and grubs and cicada larvae and everything underground, deep inside, down and in where you cannot see the life happening. Life is rich in the time of keeping still, sap flowing, cells curing, changes taking place. I will return to the great tree and be convinced once again that her branches have danced in the night, and I will know that beneath her outer black stillness there is life living deeply. Inside us all, in the depths of our winters, things are going on, things we will have no clue of until spring comes, and perhaps not even then.

Six

VIOLENCE AT SMITH'S INLET

In killing you changed death to life.

—SAINT JOHN OF THE CROSS, *THE LIVING FLAME OF LOVE*

The reservoir stretches north and south for more than twelve miles, a jewel of "managed naturalness" set in the center of a huge metropolitan area. It provides drinking water, flood control, and backup electrical power for the community. The water company maintains the surrounding watershed as a wildlife preserve, which means I have five thousand acres of wildness just a few miles from my home. I could slip my canoe into the water and suddenly be where I saw no buildings, no roads, where the quiet was palpable. And the wildlife is there: deer and foxes, skunks and raccoons, osprey, hawks, bald eagles, great blue herons, and countless others. There I have lain on my back in the canoe on a summer midday and watched a great horned owl fly over me first one way, then the other, so close I could almost touch him. There I have watched the mating, nesting, and hatching of Canada geese, and there I was attacked by a pair of bald eagles ... but I will tell that story later.

There also I have seen deer swim sweetly, softly, silently in morning mist from one shore to the other where the waters narrow, and a huge beaver who swam back and forth beneath the canoe, leaving trails of breath-bubbles as the canoe drifted by his lodge.

SQUIRREL

Greg and I even saw a squirrel swimming there once. Sitting in the front of the canoe, Greg spotted it first. "Hey Dad, what is that?" He was pointing to a long, narrow shape in the water, swimming toward the shore. I thought it might have been a snake, but it seemed to have a furry head and little ears, and it was dog-paddling rather than snaking through the water. We decided to get closer. Even up close, I didn't identify it as a squirrel. You just don't expect squirrels in the middle of reservoirs. I told Greg I thought it could be an otter or even a weasel. But he said, "Dad, do squirrels swim?"

I told him I'd never heard of such a thing, but that most animals can swim if they have to. "How'd he get way out here in the water?" Greg asked. Again I didn't have a clue. The little creature did seem to be struggling, perhaps more panicked by our approach than by the water. Tentatively, Greg extended his paddle toward the squirrel, which immediately turned and swam right toward the paddle. My first thought was of how sweet Greg was to want to rescue the squirrel. My second thought was of what it might be like to have a crazed, waterlogged squirrel in the canoe with us.

"No!" I shouted, but too late. The squirrel had grabbed Greg's paddle blade and was trying to climb up it to the handle, to the canoe. Greg looked back at me quizzically, as if wondering why I, too, would not want to save the squirrel. I said the first thing that came to mind: "That thing is going to kill us if it gets in the canoe!"

As silly as that must have sounded, Greg somehow understood. He lowered the paddle beneath the water until the squirrel floated off. Without missing a beat, the squirrel swam directly toward the canoe. "Paddle! Paddle!" I shouted.

Greg needed no encouragement. I think perhaps he'd looked into the deranged eyes of that rodent. We both paddled fiercely with the dogpaddling squirrel scrabbling along the canoe sides and then chasing us, until we finally outdistanced him. We sat catching our breath and watched the squirrel make it to shore, run across the rocky beach and up a tree. I don't know who started it, but the silence was interrupted by a snort, followed by a guffaw, followed by belly-bending peals of laughter. Greg and I still talk about nearly being killed by an aquatic squirrel.

Along this reservoir, there are several picnic areas and coves with boat-launching ramps. The one closest to my house is called Smith's Inlet. Driving down a hilly, curving road, you pass the boat ramp and then, at the very end of the inlet, you come to a picnic area and playground. Families gather there on pleasant weekends to fish, to walk along the shore, and to feed the waterfowl. From that civilized area, paths enter the woods or follow the waterside in many directions. Walk for five minutes in any direction and you're pretty much alone. It becomes very wild very quickly, and even though people leave a lot of trash around, the place is always beautiful.

Some of the paths lead to rugged, lovely fishing spots on outcroppings of rock or gentle sand beaches when the water level is down a bit. When the kids were little, long before I got my canoe, the whole family often went to the playground at the end of the inlet. Now, I never go there, and it isn't just because of my health. Even if I were in perfect shape, I would still stay away from the end of Smith's Inlet.

TURTLE

I don't remember exactly when it happened; it must have been 1978 or 1979. It was a hot and muggy summer afternoon, July or August, the water clear near the shoreline and the woods a deep, rich summertime green. The three boys and I were going fishing. Betty and Julie, never much into catching fish, had stayed home. We were making our way along one of the paths at the inlet's end, not far from the playground, heading toward a rock point on the other side where we thought the fishing might be good. We came to a fork in the path and for some reason I went uphill and, thank

God, the boys went down, closer to the water. Off to my left I noticed the remains of a small fire on a great flat rock, the usual beer cans around it. I responded habitually, with silence and disgust. *They could at least carry out their trash.* I hate trash in the woods, not so much because it hurts the environment or is unpleasant to the eye, but because I think it reflects a dedicated, though usually unconscious, human hostility toward Nature. I am certain that people leave trash in the woods not from simple carelessness but because they fear and hate wildness. I've seen people throw beer cans into the woods; they do it with vengeance.

Then something, I saw something in the middle of the rock, something set apart from the fire, something rounded, globular, moist, and still. It was a shape that registered, something I knew, but different, distorted, grotesque. I took a few steps left and stared empty-eyed at what someone had done there.

Now let me see if I can write this. Let me pray. The thing was a box turtle, dead but not long dead. Its legs were splayed out, stretched flat. Its head extended, cold chin on cold rock. A few flies buzzed. A drop of sweat ran into my eye.

What they had done, oh God, what they had done, was carve a two-inch hole in the turtle's back, in the top of the middle of the round mound shell of this living thing, down, down into its insides. Sticking out of the ghastly moist hole were the butts of four cigarettes. Filter-tipped. Two different brands.

Strange that I should notice such detail when all I wanted was to get out of there, run far away from the thing and all memory of it, get to the kids and steer them away from it, keep them from seeing it, just get us all away. But even as I backed up, even as my body and mind scrambled toward anyplace other than that immediate horror, something else in me, against my prayers and wishes and fears, was calculating, imagining what the action had been like there on that particular rock last night.

Party time. Levis and T-shirts, I guessed, no women there, probably three or four men. I couldn't imagine one person doing such a thing alone, and there were the different cigarette brands. Two people is too intimate for such an act, so it takes three, and four is even more likely because there's someone to have the idea and someone to egg him on to the terrible completion and someone to just go along with it and someone who will be horrified. Yes, four men, probably young, probably single. No females, not even playing the role of the one to be horrified, because a woman, I just believe, would not have attended or permitted that particular little stunt.

I moved out fast, suddenly a real wilderness man hopping over logs, dodging thorns, slipping between the trees back toward my boys who were, Oh God, coming my way. "Take that path there," I shouted. "It's too rough this way." Yeah, too rough, tell me about it. Earl, the oldest, kept coming toward me; I was sure he could see the rock from where he was—though not the thing that was on it. I had put my body between his eyes and the turtle. He knew something was wrong, but I said nothing more; all I could think was *God don't let him see it.* I pushed him brusquely toward the lower path. Through some mercy on God's part, or some growing wisdom in Earl, he did not resist.

We spent a while fishing. For once, I was uninterested in catching fish. I was preoccupied with two things: trying to keep the image of the turtle out of my consciousness, and trying to figure a different way to go back when it came time to go home. But there was no other way back. I would just have to keep the boys on the lower path, near the water. I could not tell them about it, tell them why I was so shaken. How could I tell anyone when I could not bear thinking about it myself?

Returning was more awful than the original encounter. I managed to keep the boys away, but passing the place was a pure experience of horror. You know what it's like to be aware of where something really bad is, and to know it's really there, and to be avoiding it, sneaking by?

It's like something in your mind that you try not to think about, only it's there and you know it even though you pretend not to, and while half of you is writhing to get away from it, the other half is right there, thinking it, chewing on it inside you.

Or maybe when you were a little child and you thought you saw something move in the dark, and you began to run, and the more you ran the more the whatever-it-was grew in the darkness behind you, chasing, closing in, and you ran faster, and it was almost upon you. That's how this was, but this was real, real in form and substance in physical space. For years afterward, the image of the thing on the rock was in my mind, just like that. And I kept trying to have it not be there.

Psychiatrically, I suppose I handled the whole thing wrong. The psychologically correct way would have been to confront the situation, face into my abhorrence, accept the ghastliness, maybe spend a little time with the turtle, perhaps even bury the thing with reverence and a few significant thoughts about human violence and prayers for healing. Rituals are supposed to help. For that matter, to really make the most of a family opportunity I could even have called my boys over and said, "See what awful things people can do?" and we could have had a little sharing about their feelings. Fat chance. It's that sort of stuff that got me tired of psychiatry.

Besides always being about management, the psychologically correct ways of handling things are often just downright impossible in the real moment. This of course makes things worse, because you know that you're upset, and you also know that you are not handling being upset in the correct way, and so you are doubly upset. This is the negative side of psychology. Like the negative side of religion, it gives you all kinds of good ways to manage your life, only you can't really do them, so you wind up feeling worse than before.

I never did handle the thing with the turtle correctly. I was never able to return to that rock, or to that path through the woods, or even to the lower path by the water. I did not return to Smith's Inlet at all for several years after the turtle. And when I did go back, I put my canoe in at the boat launch, far east of the inlet's end.

The first time I returned to the inlet, it was because I had heard rumors of good fishing there, and my fishing addiction overcame my abhorrence of the place. There were times, back then, when the possibility of catching fish could overcome just about anything. But I always stayed well away from the paths that led toward the rock. I never, ever went back to the place of the turtle.

FISH

One sunny Saturday, years later, I was fishing off the point where Smith's Inlet joins the big water. I had cast a worm into the shallows and was leaning back against a tree, waiting, lazing. Perhaps fifteen minutes had passed when I noticed the line begin to move. I softly released the bail on my reel to let the line play out. *Take it, now,* I thought. People who bottom-fish know a strangely peaceful expectancy right then, when whatever-it-is explores the bait, and everything is softly suspended, gently poised. It is all so delicate.

The line moved out slowly, tentatively at first, then steadily. It had all the signs of a catfish, my favorite, my great dinner fish. It was almost time to set the hook, and my usual thoughts of hugeness came, the possible gigantism of the fish. I flipped the bail back, waited until the line was taut, then jerked the rod to set the hook. Oh, yes, yes, it was big. It was like hooking a truck.

The familiar anticipation came, almost a fear, as I reeled the line and wondered what it was that I had wounded and was so connected with through the slender nylon filament. At such moments you can sense the life of the fish at the end of the line, a very special aliveness unique to each species. I reeled in, the drag spinning off and on, and it just did not feel like a catfish. Catfish can be very sluggish on a line, but they tend to jerk this way and that, and this thing was just swimming steadily in a straight line. It would rest awhile and I'd reel it in some, like a dead weight at the end of my line. Then it would start swimming again and there was nothing I could do but let it run; the line would break if I resisted. This was hardly a fight; it felt more like waiting for a bus. It was as if the fish did not even feel the hook, as if he were entirely unaware of it and just swimming at his pleasure, unknowingly allowing me to haul him back towards me whenever he paused.

Inside I was growing increasingly excited and a little frightened. The sheer weight of the thing thrilled me; it had to be the biggest creature I'd ever hooked in these waters. But I was afraid about what it was. Maybe it wasn't a fish at all. Perhaps it was a snapping turtle—I'd seen them nearby as big as three feet across—Oh God, don't let it be a turtle. I could not stand hooking a turtle. How could I get the hook out, even if I got the thing to shore? And if he broke the line, the thought of him swimming off with a hook in his mouth—or worse, in his throat—too much.

There was more about what might be on the end of the line. Even in fresh water, deep bait fishing is archetypal. It is about as Jungian as life can get. You cast your line into dark, unseen depths and something is alive there, and it connects, and you start to bring it to the surface, to daylight, to consciousness, and you begin to wonder if you really want to see what it is. But there it is, whatever it is, on the end of your line. Like it or not, you are connected. Committed. Enchanted.

The pulling and waiting went on for at least half an hour. I took great care not to let the line break, and after a while I really got into enjoying the pull, the swim, the getting closer, the not-knowing. Three other fishermen set down their rods and walked over to watch.

"Whatcha got there?"

"I haven't the slightest idea."

"Looks big."

"Yep."

The competitiveness of fishing is unique. It is usually implicit, unspoken, at most joked about. But it's fierce and, in its own way, deadly. At that moment, I was doing just fine. I had three guys just standing by me, their own rods forgotten, awed by my encounter with something huge and I, in excellent fisherman form, was acting as if it happened every day.

Finally I saw its shape. A fishy shape, definitely not a turtle, thank God, nor any shadowy psychomonster from my nightmares. Just a really big fish, the kind I always hope to catch. I stepped back to reach for my net, and one of the fishermen handed it to me. Being helpful is part of the game.

"Catfish, I hope," I said casually. "Carp maybe."

"Yeah, carp. Big one."

"Yeah."

"Gonna keep him?"

"Not if it's a carp."

"Yeah. Whatcha fishing with?"

"Worms. Deep."

"Uh-huh. I'm using minnows."

Fishers who use minnows are a class above those of us who use worms. But at the moment I was the one with the big fish, and that's what finally counts. At the end of everything, on judgment day, it's the absolute size of your fish that determines the value of your life.

The fish lazed over on its side in the shallow water, exposing round bronze scales the size of quarters. It was a carp. I was a little disappointed that it wasn't a catfish; I'd had some thoughts about broiling catfish steaks. But it was big, truly, wonderfully, breath-stoppingly big. And, to my human judgment, it was also stupid. Right up until I got him on shore, this carp did not seem to understand that he was on the end of a line, that there was a hook in his tender mouth, and that if he had been a catfish he would have been doomed. He was far too big for the net but I was able to use it to lever him onto the sand, and there he just lay glistening in the sun, great fishy eyes seemingly unperturbed, unknowing of anything. The other fishermen walked away in silence, and I opened my tackle box to get my disposable camera. I took a picture of the fish and then got my pliers to remove the hook.

Carps' mouths are soft and delicate compared with those of most other fish, and I tried to be careful getting the hook out. As I pried, he jerked, flopped, flipped over and knocked the pliers out of my hand. I tried again, holding the pliers tight, trying with my other hand to keep him still, and again he flopped, and the hook came out, but there was a sickening cracking sound and blood and I saw that I had broken his jaw. Horror inside me. Horror like the turtle. Something in me at that very moment, something swamped with guilt, wanted desperately to blame the fish for flopping over, just as perpetrators of violent crimes often blame their victims. I was just trying to get the hook out; he shouldn't have jerked like that. But the facts were indisputable: I caught the fish with a hook in his tender mouth and then I took his picture while he was laid out vulnerable in the sun and then I broke his jaw.

Could he survive? I had no idea. Carp are bottom feeders and quite primitive, whatever that means. Maybe he would make it. Probably not. I did not feel good inside. I did not feel good at all. I lifted him back into the water as gently as possible, with great tenderness, as if that would make a difference. I even told him I was sorry, so sorry. I listened to my heart, which was quietly asking forgiveness from God and the fish. I was on my knees in the cool water as I let him slip out of my hands, wanting the water to be gentle for him, wanting something healing for his jaw and my spirit. He swam off, lazily, steadily, as if nothing had happened. But something had.

I understood something about our daughter Julie's drug addiction. My fishing addiction was a milder form of the same thing. I had killed so many fish, wounded so many others, but I kept doing it. It always bothered me, but I kept doing it. It was perhaps fifteen minutes, maybe half an hour, before my mind was able to do its denials and rationalizations. Then I put another worm on the hook, cast it out, leaned back against the tree as the afternoon sun glinted from small waves and the reflected light flickered among the leaves.

DUCK

The following spring, after a completely uneventful day of fishing off the same point, I was walking back along the shoreline toward my car. As I approached the launching ramp, I noticed a commotion in the water and a small gathering of people on the shore. Some of them were shouting, and a couple of young men were throwing rocks at a swan that was swimming in circles about twenty feet from the shore. I ran forward, hoping to stop them before they hit the swan, but then I saw what was really happening.

Slowly, steadily, the swan was in the process of killing a duck. I couldn't tell what kind of duck it was, only that it was very small, very frail. In a supremely dedicated way, the swan was drowning it. The swan swam over the duck again and again, using his breast and feet to keep the duck under himself, underwater, for as long as possible. As soon as the duck escaped to catch a breath and utter a tiny squawk, the swan would submerge it again. The duck was exhausted, disoriented, nearly dead, too far gone to be frantic yet still reflexively grasping and gasping for the surface, for air, for life.

The guys throwing stones were trying to save the duck, but the swan seemed unfazed, even unaware of their attack. He was dead set in his purpose, implacable, relentless, and terrifyingly calm. The drowning took a very long time. Perhaps if the duck had not lost its bearings it might have made for shore, but instead it moved farther and farther out into the water, its pursuer never once letting it rest. The two were finally beyond rock-throwing distance and the small group of people slowly dispersed. No one said a word. What was there to say? I have no idea what they felt, what was in their minds, except that it was not a good moment for any of us.

I stayed. I watched. At first I tried to explain it. Could the swan be defending a territory? I did not understand how any bird could establish a territory there where so many birds of different species congregated to feed. And with so many other, bigger birds around, why pick on this tiny frail creature of a duck? Was the duck wounded, perhaps, or sick? Was this some survival-of-the-fittest mission the swan was instinctively performing? Reasoning was hopeless, but I wanted there to be a reason. I *needed* a reason.

The swan, it appeared, needed no reason at all. I couldn't avert my eyes from him. He was so patient, so supremely dedicated, unswerving, steadfast in the killing. There seemed to be neither hostility nor mercy in him—only the steady, calm, drawn-out process of the drowning. I wondered why he did not strike the duck with his beak or hit him with his wings; I had seen angry swans do that in the past. I could not help but feel he did not strike the duck because to do so would have hastened the death, and this particular death was to be slow, a torture-death by drowning.

It is difficult to refrain from attributing motives to animals; we so desperately need their behavior to make some kind of human sense. I think it has to do with knowing, down deep, that much of our own behavior doesn't make sense either. We really want there to be good reasons somewhere. For me to admit that there may have been no sense, no motive for the swan's deadly play is to admit that such violence, such destructiveness can *just happen*. It would be like so much of Nature, just what it is. And that means it can be that way in human beings as well.

So I stood alone where the parents had shuffled their children away, where the young men had left in silence, and I looked far out into the water and watched the swan finish killing the duck. Or perhaps I watched the duck die under the relentless persever-ance of the swan. Or maybe I watched the water and the sky, within the embrace of which, during those long, long moments, some ripples and feathers simply churned. To me, it was an emotional eternity until finally the duck no longer surfaced. The swan swam in slow circles there for a while—I would say to make sure the duck was really dead, but that's a human reason—and then he took his place again among the other swans and the geese and the ducks at the upper end of the inlet, near to the picnic grounds, where the children were again happily throwing bread crumbs. See the pretty swan.[8]

HUMAN

After refinishing my canoe during the winter of 1993, Paul and I put it in at Smith's Inlet on Easter weekend. We were going fishing. It turned out to be what we call a typical May-boy fishing trip—tangling our lines, snarling our reels, hooking each other repeatedly, but not catching a single fish. But it felt wonderful to paddle out across the water that first spring morning. The air continued to carry the chill of winter, and the water, still cold enough to be dangerous, remained winter-quiet, barely awakening to the possibilities of spring. The trees and undergrowth along the shores were still bare; only the slightest misting of green buds ghosted around their trunks and branches.

Usually when I fished, and especially when I fished with my boys, we were very interested in catching something. But this day was different. Paul and I knew we were unlikely to catch anything that early in the year—and we couldn't keep bass anyway, not until June 15. We just wanted to experience being out in the canoe that I had worked on so faithfully and lovingly all winter.

For the most part it was a pure outdoors-enjoyment day, uncramped by the need to catch fish. I made coffee in my usual canoe way—dumping instant from a plastic bag into a cup, filling it with hot water from my thermos. We talked some, felt the water, the smoothness of the canoe's freshly refinished bottom as it glided across the reservoir. I thought of mists and emptiness. We saw no other people and, as expected, caught no fish. We were just in the spring water-sky with the early herons, terns, an occasional osprey. A beautiful day, a lovely time. Sweet. When I dropped Paul off at his house he said, "Thanks, Dad. Felt really good."

A few days later, Paul called me about something else and before hanging up said, "Oh, did you hear they found a body out there at Smith's Inlet? Must have happened about the same time we were there."

The newspaper had a brief report the next day. It was a young woman in her twenties, apparently beaten to death. Her body had been found Easter Tuesday, floating near the shore about fifty feet west of the launching ramp. A fisherman had found it. I thought about how he must have felt and was glad it wasn't me. The report gave no further information. It was on a back page. An unknown woman's murder isn't very big news around here anymore.

A week later, as I was putting the canoe into the water at the ramp, a county policeman drove up and parked over by the portable toilets. I wondered if it had anything to do with the murder, but the officer looked very casual as he got out and stretched. He ambled over toward me.

"How ya doin' today?" he said, looking up and down the waterside.

"Pretty good. Just getting ready to go out." I realized I was
explaining myself. Why is it every time I see a cop I begin to act
as if I'd done something wrong?

"Man, I'd sure like to be goin' out instead of working. I just
drive down here to check it out sometimes, see what the fishing
might be like."

"So you do some fishing here, huh?" I asked. That's another
thing. Neither of us, I guess, would outright acknowledge that
we might come here for some reason other than fishing, like just
to bask in the beauty, even though I suspect that's exactly what
he was up to. Men are like that sometimes. We can't just *be* someplace—we have to be there for a reason: fishing, hunting, going
somewhere, *doing* something.

"I'm down here pretty much every day I have off. Caught a
three-pound pike last weekend. They're up in the shallows now.
God, I wish I didn't have to work today."

"Bet you got a rod and reel in the trunk," I smiled.

"Naw, not allowed. Besides, I use a boat." Another aspect of
the competition is that boat fishermen rank higher than shore
fishermen. A canoe doesn't quite count as a boat, but it was close
enough so we could talk.

"You hear anything about that body they found out here?" I
asked. I was putting stuff into the canoe, acting like I was just
making conversation, but I really wanted to know.

"Naw, not really. They did get a suspect, though. Boyfriend
or something. Picked him up down south, one of the Carolinas

I think. They're extraditing him back to the county. What you fishing with?"

My humble truth would now have to come out.

"Worms." I said it assertively. Because he'd caught a pike, I knew he used artificial lures. That ranked him close to the top of the fishing hierarchy, only a notch or two below fly fishers. I tried to explain. "Mostly I go for catfish. Love to eat 'em."

"Yeah, they're okay." He started back toward his car, still ambling, but the conversation was clearly over. He'd lost all interest when he heard I used worms.

"See ya," I said to his back.

"Yep. Good luck."

SMITH'S INLET

Turtle, fish, duck, human: four focused episodes of violence that happened to four different species during fifteen years in a few acres of woods and water called Smith's Inlet. During that time countless other violences happened there that I did not witness. Hundreds of thousands of fish were killed at Smith's Inlet by birds and bigger fish, by storms and chemicals and fishermen. Tens of thousands of birds were killed by other birds, by snakes, by their own mothers, by starvation and disease. Millions of insects ate one another. Scores of human parents screamed and struck their children at the picnic grounds. Each year, hundreds of box turtles were crushed beneath car wheels on the road that runs around the inlet, and their eggs were devoured by raccoons and possums, and their babies were eaten by predator birds. Maybe another person was killed there, or raped, and probably some other small animals were tortured to death in one way or another. I don't know.

When I told a friend my Smith's Inlet stories he said, "That sounds like a good place to stay away from!" But there's no special curse on Smith's Inlet; no demonic mystery resides there. Apart from its beauty, there's nothing special at all about the place. You could take any other few acres anywhere and if you had the courage to look closely at the violence that happened there over time, it could overwhelm you. Violence happens everywhere. Smith's Inlet is simply a place where many creatures, including human beings, find themselves interacting. It's only special to me because it has become a prism, a consciousness-crystal that makes me focus on violence that I do not want to look at. Mainly, it's still because of the turtle.

MEMORY

It has always been the turtle that has stuck in my mind. Over the years two scenes kept trying to get into my consciousness. The first was the actual memory of what I had seen: the image of the defiled creature on the rock amid the beer cans, the cigarette butts sticking out of it, the flies. The second was my imagination of how it might have happened, a vague picture of four young men sitting on the rock around the not-yet-dead turtle with their beer and cigarettes, one of them holding a knife. I would sense their eyes looking at the turtle and glancing briefly at one another. I would imagine sweat drops on their faces, but I never saw their expressions and I never imagined what they might have said to one another. When such scenes crept into my mind I usually fought them off, but now and then I would take a breath and face into them. When I was able to do this—sometimes gripping the arms of my chair—other memories followed. They came in waves, with horrible abundance. The dead turtle became the sacrificial symbol of all the violence that had been a part of my life.

First there were memories from Vietnam, of fighter jocks swaggering after a mission, bragging of elephants or water buffaloes they'd brought down with their machine guns.

"Can't kill gooks, gotta kill something."

"You shoulda seen that baby fall. I must have took off half his hind side and he was still flopping around."

And other things from the war, especially the high keening wail of Vietnamese peasant women crying over their dead. I can still hear their cry in the back of my head, a sound like no other I have ever heard. It is high and shrill and plaintive and it makes me imagine the scream of bleeding mountains.

The memory comes. It is a sweltering summer morning at Cam Ranh Bay and I am standing next to a surgeon on the hospital loading dock. We are smoking cigarettes and watching a helicopter land; rotor-blown sand is biting our faces. No more than five feet to our right, hunkered down against the steel guardrails of the dock, two Vietnamese women are sobbing-screeching over a dead child. The surgeon takes his eyes off the chopper and looks at the women and says, almost in their faces as if he were commenting on the weather, he says to me, "Death doesn't mean much to them. They take it in stride. Reincarnation or something like that."

"Then why do they cry so?" I ask very gently. "Why do they cry so?" But his eyes are back on the chopper and its sound blows my words away and there's nothing more to say anyway.[9]

I'm off duty, so I hitch a jeep ride over the dunes to the impeccable beach on the South China Sea where brass casings of rockets glint underwater in the sunlight among tropical fish, and where the high rocks to the north toward Nha Trang sprout old Japanese pillboxes, decaying from another war long past, or perhaps just an earlier phase of this war, which has never really ended.

And memories of trying to sleep and stay awake at the same time in my flak jacket and helmet in the corner of my hootch. There were two kinds of times I did that: when the base was under attack and when the American GIs were partying, high on slammer cocktails of beer and marijuana and pure white heroin up their noses and careening between the hootches with their grenades and M-16s and it would be nothing unusual if a couple of them decided in their blurred rage to take out some officers. Relatively speaking, I hardly feared the enemy. No one was sure who the enemy was anyway. And at least someone who's an enemy must have reasons for his or her violence, or so you'd think.

And memories of so many stories of violence from my prison work that I neither need nor desire to recount here. To do so would be, to use a term, overkill. Suffice it to say I worked for two years as a psychiatrist at a maximum security prison with people convicted of repeated violent crimes. There everything was embraced in the unique retrospective logic of human violence: "It wasn't my fault she got shot. I told her not to move and she moved, so I shot her. It was her fault." Like me and the carp; he shouldn't have flopped over like that.

The turtle, that blessed sacred creature on its unwilling altar, also brought back memories of many violences I committed myself, from childhood fights to adult outbursts of sarcasm and scorn against my family and colleagues, the harsh derision I used to call humor, my competitiveness, rebellion, envy, on and on.

The turtle treated me to an endless slide show of destruction, and it nearly overwhelmed me. I have heard that native people of the Arctic have many words for snow, each describing a different quality. I think we could do the same for violence. There's completely accidental violence, violence that comes from carelessness, reasoned and premeditated violence, impulsive violence, violence for sport, mindless violence under its own unknown power, and pure cruelty, evil for evil's sake. And there's revenge, the only thing that fully defends us against grief. And there's jealousy, paranoia, self-abuse, self-defense, predation, genocide, political torture, bigotry, children pulling the wings off flies, homophobia, rape, lynching. And there's what we call natural violence: hurricanes, tornadoes, earthquakes, plagues.

My mind still cries out, *Why?*

And the emptiness of consciousness replies, *Because it is.*

REASONS

Philosophers have tried to find reasons for the destructiveness inherent in Nature, and theologians have pondered how innocent people can suffer when God is supposed to be benevolent and all-powerful. Behavioral scientists have sought out motivations for human violence and have come up with countless theories: anger internalized, pent-up, unexpressed, boiling over. Neurological abnormalities. Misfirings in the temporal lobe of the brain. The violence of television and video games. Neurotransmitter imbalance. Seizures. Some abused children grow up violent; some do not. Sociopathy. Primitive impulses inherited from our forebears. Tribal warfare, feuds, archetypal animosities, economics, political power. Eating the hearts of one's enemies to gain their spirit strength. Man's deep resentment against woman and the Earth that bore him into existence, his fear of Anima, his true inner self, the threat to his power that Nature and women present.

For me, thinking about the reasons for violence is like a Mayboy fishing trip. I'm in the canoe with one of my sons and we're both obsessed with catching fish, each of us using two or three rods, sometimes with more than one hook on a line, and maybe a throw line for catfish as well. It's never more than a minute or two before our lines are snarled and what you think is a bite is just the other guy pulling on his line, which is entangled with yours, making him think he has a bite of his own. This is how my mind feels when I try to understand the reasons for violence:

thoughts tossed out every which way, lines leading here and there, all snarled up. And, of course, not catching a damn thing.

The last time I understood human violence was my first year of psychiatry training. After that, I kept finding exceptions and contradictions: people I thought would be violent were not, and people I thought would not be, were. The more experience I had, the less I knew.

During my time in institutional psychiatry, I was often called to court to testify about violence. Everyone wants certainty, but nobody wants it more than those in the legal system. The courts want to know whether a person is mentally responsible for a violent act, whether a person who has committed violent acts is likely to do them again, whether someone has been cured of the disorder that supposedly caused his or her violence. Psychiatrists are the experts in such matters, expected to know the answers. I always tried to be as helpful as possible, but I also tried to be honest. A lawyer would ask, "Now, doctor, in your professional opinion, is this person likely to be violent in the future?"

"Well, he's been violent in the past. Maybe he will be again."

"But what's your professional opinion about the possibility?"

"I'm sorry, but that's it. I really don't know."

Then the judge would intervene. "Can you be more specific, doctor? You have examined this man."

"Yes, but I can't predict what he's going to do in the future."

The way it usually went, I'd tell them about the studies showing that the only meaningful predictor of people's future behavior is their past behavior, and even that isn't certain because people really can change. Those in charge of the legal system just couldn't believe—or refused to accept—that we didn't know more than that. For my part, I rather enjoyed being an expert witness who didn't know much of anything, but the lawyers didn't like it at all. A defense lawyer once got so angry with my lack of certainty about his client's potential for violence that he threw a set of keys at me. The keys missed me and hit the judge's bench, and the lawyer, for his violence, was taken out in handcuffs and cited for contempt of court.

It was especially poignant in jury trials. The silent stillness of the jury was always spooky to me; I never knew what the jurors felt. I wanted to believe that some of them appreciated my honesty; a few at least must have found it refreshing to have a supposedly competent professional acknowledge the limitations of his knowledge. I think we all know, at some level, that psychologists and psychiatrists can't predict violence any better than economists can predict recessions or the government can predict international crises. We do desperately *want* someone to know—we want the feeling of control that such knowing would bring—but down deep I think we're aware that with all our scientific explanations we still live in mystery. Sometimes I think hearing it admitted outright must come as a relief.

It's understandable that we want reasons: the more we know about something, the more we can predict what's going to happen, the more in control we can be. And the less vulnerable. The word *vulnerable* literally means "capable of being wounded." When it comes to violence, knowledge is like a shield that makes us less "woundable." Quite rightly, then, we collect as much knowledge as we can to predict hazards and protect ourselves against them.

The problem is that we go crazy with it. We act as if we can know enough to be completely invulnerable, just as I did when I first went into the wild alone. I made lists of things to protect me from all possible dangers. A little such preparation makes sense, but I overdid it; I tried to foresee so many dangers that I became paranoid, suspicious, and mistrustful of the very Nature I wanted to join.

We can discern some partial reasons for some violence, and these can help us take reasonable precautions. Not surprisingly, most of these reasons are not profound scientific discoveries; they're just common sense. When wild animals attack people, for example, it's usually because they feel threatened in some way, so it's generally wise not to threaten them more. For the most part, the same thing is true of human violence. Human motives of revenge and power may be more complex, but still they are often understandable, and such understanding can make our responses more effective.

Yet there remain within Nature, within animals, and within human beings, levels of violence that will always be a mystery, dimensions of destructiveness that will forever appear random and mindless no matter how much research we do. In our compulsion to be invulnerable, we find this difficult to admit. We are so desperate to have reasons for violence that we consider "random acts of violence" or "mindless destruction" as being worse than reasoned, premeditated violence. But think about it—does having a reason really make it better?

We seem to accept a certain random, mindless quality in "natural" violence: tornadoes, hurricanes, earthquakes, floods, and the like. And we don't expect viruses to have reasons for infecting us; we understand that it's just their nature—it's what they do. We wisely want to learn as much as we can about such things, to help protect ourselves from them, but most people accept that we're never going to learn enough to have absolute control over them.

On the other hand, we still desperately want to believe that the violence of "higher" animals, and certainly of human beings, must always have decipherable reasons. Many people, for example, still believe the myth that we are the only animals that kill for pure enjoyment, although repeated studies have revealed numerous acts of violence among nonhuman animals that have nothing to do with predation or territory protection: violence for no reason other than enjoyment. Why do cats torture the mice and birds they catch before killing them? Why did the swan kill the duck? And why did he do it in such a slow, dedicated, implacable way? Why do some of the most peaceful, passive, united-with-nature aboriginal human beings still torture animals before they kill them? Some of us will cling to the belief that there is always a rational explanation and that eventually, with enough good scientific research, we'll learn what it is and be able to control it. Dream on.

The research should continue. We should do what we can to minimize our own violence. I would say we haven't even begun to realize how violent we are to one another, to other species, to the earth, even to ourselves, and the more we can comprehend and control our violence, the better. But within and around us there will always remain a violence that just is, just exists, just happens.

It is a quality of destructiveness that is completely wild, unreasoned, unforgiving, relentless, and inexplicable.

Until we accept this shadow side of ourselves and of the world around us, a mystery that contains destruction as well as creation, we will never be able to appreciate being an integral part of things. We will always see ourselves as separate. If we want to be a part of Nature instead of apart from it, we must make friends with a mystery that is both joyous and horrifying, and this will never happen as long as we're obsessed with explaining and controlling everything.

I have read that when wolves encircle an isolated caribou, a variety of things can happen. If the caribou runs, the wolves will almost surely chase it down and kill it. More often, the caribou will stop, exhausted perhaps, and stand still. The wolves pause also, waiting. At some point the caribou, apparently sensing the impossibility of escape, looks right into the eyes of the wolves. The eyes of predator and prey meet. In this moment, which may last a long time, something happens. Sometimes, after the eye-meeting, the wolves attack and kill. Other times, they simply turn around and walk away.[10]

Special moments like that happen sometimes between predators and prey. They can happen in war also, and in robberies and rapes. Eyes meet, and something encounters something, something *connects*, and it makes a mysterious difference. I am convinced that no matter how much research we do, we will never understand what goes on in such encounters. I have talked at length with human predators, men convicted of repeated violent crimes. Occasionally they speak with quiet voices about the intimacy of their encounters with their victims. I do not understand it, and neither do they. Sometimes, though, they seem almost reverent.

BONES

I do not know whether it is a similar thing, but I feel a sense of reverent connection when I touch the bones of an animal that has died in the wild. It is much more than acknowledging life and death. It seems not even to happen in my mind, but rather in the cells of my body, in the flesh of my hand as I touch a bone, hold it, feel its texture and its vulnerability. I can't explain anything about it, but there is one brief story I can tell, of the way I was healed from the wound of the turtle. It has to do with letting myself be led.

During the years that I guided wilderness retreats, I always suggested that people let themselves be led rather than setting off with a particular place to go or agenda to meet. We would pray a little together, and then go out into the woods and fields to see what happened. In the evening we would gather to tell stories of our experiences. On one such occasion, several people told of coming upon the carcasses of deer. One woman had brought back three or four vertebrae and a leg bone. A man told of finding an almost perfect skeleton of a fawn, which looked as though its neck might have been broken. He said he did not touch the bones but just looked at them for a long, long time.

For some reason, as I heard these stories I found myself wishing that I, too, had come upon some bones. I asked the man to tell me where he had found the fawn's skeleton. He gave me the best directions he could, and at sunrise the next morning I set off to find it. I searched the area he had described but found nothing. I felt frustration growing but then remembered my words to the group: let yourself be led. I gave up, relaxed, followed where my feet seemed to take me. Maybe I said a little prayer.

No more than five minutes had passed when I looked down and saw, next to my foot, not the deer skeleton, but the perfectly preserved shell of a box turtle. It was just the carapace, the round mound of the back-shell, exactly the size, shape, and color of the mutilated one I had encountered some fifteen years earlier and fifteen miles to the south at Smith's Inlet. At first I cringed inside, but as I looked at the shell it welcomed me with its perfection, its unbroken wholeness, its absolutely gentle beauty. I felt no fear, just the open sense of being here, just now, just with what is.

I squatted on my heels beside the shell and thought-felt, *If I can reach out and touch it, if I can hold it in my hand, something will be healed. The horror of the turtle will be gone inside me.* I touched the shell. It was dry, light, vulnerable, perfect. It was warm from the early morning sun. I picked it up, turned it over, brushed off some dirt, passed my fingers over its papery dry roundness. There was nothing in my mind then, no understanding, no comprehension. Nothing more was needed.

After a long time I stood, holding the shell gently against my stomach, and started to walk back. I had gone about twenty feet when I found the skeleton of the fawn with the broken neck. Like the man who had discovered it before me, I stopped and looked at it for a while, and left it undisturbed.

I brought the turtle's shell home with me, and it still rests in a special place on my bookshelf. Sometimes I just sit and hold it in my hands. Whenever I do that, my mind becomes quiet, still, and free, and I give thanks once again for my healing.

Seven

A PERFECTION
OF TREES

It was downright stupid to wear cowboy boots to the mountain
in the snow. They provide no traction at all. But it hadn't been
snowing at home and shoes were the last thing on my mind because I was leaving fast. I needed to get away.

I didn't usually go into the wild to get away from something.
Most of the time it was that familiar growing yearning and feeling of rightness that it was time to go. On this occasion, however,
I knew I was escaping. It wasn't a longing that drew me, but a
pressure that drove me. You don't have to be a psychiatrist to
know the difference.

It was the end of a particularly awful week in a February from hell. I had been surrounded by negativity for the whole month. I had disappointed several people, hurt them, made them angry. I had been selfish and inconsiderate. I felt responsible for all of it, a failure at everything. I needed to escape.

I left on Friday after work; I just pulled on the stupid boots, threw some winter things into the car, and took off. It was too late in the day to make it all the way to my really wild mountain. I just planned to get to Catoctin or Cunningham Falls, regular parks but out there, far enough away from friends and family, home and work. I brought the tent, hoping to find a campground open in the winter, but by the time I got to the mountains it was dark and I was exhausted so I bought a six-pack and signed into a cheap motel for the night. I turned on the television, flopped on the bed, drank beer, and felt crummy. I tried to pray, but all that came out was "Help." Looking back, I guess that's about as good and honest as prayer can be, but at the time it felt like yet another failure. I was a bum, a heel, a worthless fake of a person. I was no good at work, no good for my family or friends, just causing trouble for the people I loved, and I couldn't even come up with a decent prayer. It was a perfection of awfulness, feeling that way and lying in a dumpy motel room in my cowboy boots, drinking beer with the old black-and-white television sputtering. During the night I heard snow and sleet crackling on the roof and on the pavement outside.

In the morning I was up before first light, feeling better. Maybe it was the good night's sleep, but mainly I think it was the promise of the snowfall, the freshness of it, and knowing that I'd soon be fully in it, on a mountainside among the trees. I picked up a breakfast at a McDonald's drive-through and headed up the mountain road. It was early enough that the road hadn't been plowed so I had sufficient excuse to kick in the four-wheel drive on my little Blazer. It always made me feel more potent to do that. The engine whined with the extra stress and I finished off the hash browns and sipped on Styrofoam coffee and thought it was all pretty wonderful. Another perfection, much better than the awful perfection of the previous night.

I think you know what the feeling of perfection is. It just happens; you're driving along or walking along or maybe just sitting there and suddenly, gently, everything is perfect. It doesn't matter whether things are pleasant or unpleasant, or whether you're happy or sad; you just get this sense that everything, just as it is, is exactly the way it should be. It has a cleanness to it, a simplicity, a just-is-ness, an absolute sufficiency. I've now come to believe that every moment, every single moment in every single situation is really that way. It's not a matter of one moment or situation being more perfect than another; it's just a gift to have a moment's experience of the perfection that is there all the time. That's what I believe now, but I didn't then. Then it seemed I had found a perfect moment, four-wheeling in the snow drinking coffee, or perhaps one had found me, or maybe, God forgive me, I might have even thought I'd achieved it myself by getting to the right place at the right time.

I drove for a while, trying to decide where the most privacy might be, but with the snow and the early hour no one else was around, so I pulled into a public parking lot near Cunningham

Falls. I was out immediately, grabbing my backpack, making a quick check of the car, locking the door, and I was off. At my first step, I slipped and fell in the snow. Right there in the parking lot in maybe an inch of snow, my slick-soled cowboy boots went out from under me and ended a perfect moment that I had thought might turn into a perfect day. I wasn't hurt, except that in my opinion perfection had come to an end. I was already wet and cold, only a foot or two from the car. I felt stupid for wearing the cowboy boots. And even though there was no one else around, no cars in the parking lot, not even footprints, I felt humiliated. There's a world of difference between being humble and being humiliated, and this was humiliation. Outdoor woodsman Jerry, wilderness man, on his butt in a parking lot wearing cowboy boots in an inch of snow. How quickly things change.

I got back into the car, dug out my walking stick, and found another scarf to put on. Then, taking much more care, I began trudging up the hill. In the woods the snow was maybe six inches deep, traction was easier, but the going was rough. Lifting my legs high to get uphill through the snow, and digging my boot heels in so I wouldn't slip, I was winded within ten minutes. Then my mind really kicked in. So stupid for wearing the cowboy boots. So out of shape to get breathless so quickly, not taking care of my body, no exercise, smoking and drinking and not watching what I eat, sloppy person. Every morning all my neighbors are out jogging while I'm sitting and smoking and drinking one cup of coffee after another and writing psychospiritual junk on my computer, acting like I know something worthwhile. Now here I am all winded and breathing the cold air so fast it hurts my lungs and it would serve me right if I had a heart attack right here on this damn mountainside and if the snow covered me up and no one found my body for a long, long time. Then they'd miss me, but it would probably be good riddance anyway because I can't do anything right. And would they miss me, really?

I'd lived long enough and practiced enough psychiatry to know that such thoughts get on a track and, like a train going downhill, they just go on and on with a momentum hurtling into sickening self-absorption. They never, ever lead to anything but more of themselves. I recognized what I was doing to myself, and of course that made me feel even worse. Not only was I stupid and worthless and out of shape, but now I was feeling sorry for myself. So I forged on before I'd really caught my breath, going to find some place, some beautiful place in the snow, just to sit, just to be, maybe to pray, hopefully to stop this mental craziness and heal, please, be healed.

I attacked the rest of the hill like a crazed warrior. I fell down three or four times and grabbed the snow and fought it and broke tree branches pulling on them to get up and didn't care a bit about being out of breath. I was sweating inside the coldness, giving myself to the pure strenuousness of making it to wherever I was going, which wasn't really anywhere. It felt good to know the liveliness that can come from pitting oneself against Nature. Nature is willing for that, willing to become an imaginary enemy so you can think you know who you are for a little while because you think you know what you're fighting. Nature is willing for anything.

Halfway up the hill, immersed in the struggle for the top, I remembered a photograph in the last issue of my college alumni magazine. It showed some members of the class of 1953 who, having apparently searched awhile to find something significant about their graduating year, were holding a banner that said: 1953—MOUNT EVEREST CONQUERED! I wondered what Mount Everest had done that made it need to be conquered; why was it an enemy? Yeah, I know. Because it was there.

That's the point, I guess. If something is just there, getting along fine without us, neither threatening us nor needing our help, it's likely to drive us nuts. And such a thing is perfect for someone who is in need of pushing their own edge, of seeing how far they can stretch themselves. It becomes the enemy, the obstacle, the hurdle to be overcome. As I say, Nature is very willing for this. It doesn't care. If we want to separate ourselves from the natural world and turn it into something to be conquered—or cared for—it's very accommodating. It will be anything we need it to be. So this snowy hillside was willing to become my little Everest in the Appalachian foothills. At the top I leaned against my walking stick, heaving breath-clouds into the cold air.

I had a cave in mind, a rock overhang, a place out of the wind where I could sit and empty my mind. I suppose I'll never learn that such intentions almost never come true. God in the wild is full of surprises, and seems to love it immensely. I could not find a cave or an overhang anywhere, and I did not want to spend the whole day slipping and sliding around the hillside, so I settled myself against a flat upright rock that at least shielded me from the wind. I placed my plastic ground cloth on the snow next to the rock and sat down cross-legged next to my backpack.

Here I am. Thoughts that had paused during the climb uphill now recovered their strength and hit me with renewed ugliness. All my faults, my total inability to do anything right. I looked around, wanting to find something healing in the trees, in the snow, in the distant sound of a waterfall, but there was nothing except cold. Cold seeped up through the plastic into my body. I prayed for relief, for peace. It started to snow again, the hard freezing sleety snow that makes cracking sounds as it strikes you. The wind picked up and shifted around to catch me from the north. I was going to freeze there. I got up and started moving again.

I quit worrying about what to do, just followed my feet, and must have walked nearly another mile in the snowfall, beyond the sound of water, into the barren trees. Because I was no longer trying for anything, a pace of walking came to me, a gait not antagonistic to the hillside, a rhythm compatible, even harmonious, with the snow and my cowboy boots and my out-of-shape heart and lungs. As I walked, my mind stopped harassing itself and peacefulness came again—a peacefulness born of the sweet absence of harsh thoughts and the perfect presence of everything around me just being. Such times just happen. There's no way to make them happen. All you can do, I guess, is put yourself in places where they might happen, want them enough so that the wanting becomes a prayer even if you can't pray it, and just do what comes naturally.

I found myself on a gentler path that led me gradually down one hillside and very slowly up another, deeper into the trees that were blurred by snowflakes yet still stark skeletons of black and gray in winter emptiness. The park people had marked the trail with pink paint on the tree trunks. I had no idea where the path went, needed no thought of where I was going. There were no other footprints. I was alone. The falling ice-snow had formed a crust that crunched with each step. A memory came, or a series of them, of walking in the snow in Michigan when I was a teenager. It was colder there, and the snow creaked more than crunched, and my inner feeling was different too. Then, it seemed, I was always going someplace, always doing something. Now, thank God, I was going no place, doing nothing, just walking, being. A gift-sense of freedom came, a blessing-moment of Presence without agenda or intention.

I got a little high from it, intoxicated with freedom and emptiness. It wasn't quite joy, but it was close. I thought I heard something in the wind. It sounded like children laughing. It *was* children laughing, real children, a lot of real children. I couldn't see them yet, but they were coming toward me, fast. A horde.

Like everything, the laughter of children is what you make of it. If you're in the right frame of mind, it's music. When you're trying to concentrate on something else, it's noise. If your mood is right on the edge of depression as mine was, and you're just beginning to feel a bit of precious freedom in the silence of snow falling in sweet abandoned aloneness, then the laughter of children can be the most repulsive sound in the universe.

I desperately wanted to get away from those kids, get out of sight. To the east was a long flat expanse of snow and boulders among the trees. Nothing for me there. To the west the hillside rose abruptly, but a tiny lavender-marked trail indicated it must be passable, at least in good weather. I took off, leaving interesting cowboy boot tracks in the snow. Huffing up the hill I glanced off to my right, behind a fallen tree, and saw . . . yes, it was a cave, just the sort of thing I'd started out looking for. I had to climb under the horizontal tree trunk and again found myself stumbling and scrambling, pitting myself against the landscape. Clumsily I made it into the little hole in the hill. It was formed by boulders right, left, and above, and there was just enough room for me to sit on a rock with my feet stretched out to rest on another rock. I could look out from this tiny cavern, over the fallen tree that hid its entrance, down upon the trail I had been walking. It was, I realized then, another perfection, and one I would never have found had I not been escaping the oncoming sounds of the children.

They came. Looking down the hillside from my hidden spot, I could see there were about fifteen of them, maybe seven to ten years old, boys and girls, poor kids, poorly clothed, probably brought out from the inner city by some organization for a weekend of winter camping at Cunningham Falls. There was one adult with them, a shepherd with his flock of sheep gone wild; the kids were everywhere. One little boy headed up toward me, calling out to a friend that he had found a trail. He got within fifty feet of me when the adult called him back. I heard him mutter "Shit," and I wondered briefly what he would have thought, and what I would have done, if he'd stumbled upon me in my little cave. I guess I would have said "Hi." As he trudged back down the trail I noticed he was wearing sneakers. Cold wet sneakers in the snow. Better traction than my cowboy boots, but his feet must have been freezing. He was as steady as a mountain goat on that hillside. I decided I liked him. A lot.

The children moved erratically down the trail below me, shouting and laughing. Once I realized I was not going to be seen, I began to like the sound of their voices. It blended in amazing harmony with the sweet crackle of the snow in the wind, with the occasional song of a bird. It was right that the children were there; they were as much a part of the mountainside as the trees and I were, and it was good. I realized how quickly my feelings toward them had changed. Mood—or is it attitude?—colors everything. And moods and attitudes shift like the wind. I'm old enough now not to take them too seriously.

The sounds of the children's voices grew fainter in the snow, and the snow grew heavier, and the heaviness of it lay on the trees and the rocks and made me feel somehow protected. But I had been sitting very still for a long time, and the cold had gotten into my bones. I opened my backpack and took out a little can of Sterno and set it in the hole in the rock beneath my legs. It took a couple of matches to get it lit because my hands were shaking now with the coldness. Then the warmth came up under my knees and I took off my sodden gloves and warmed my hands and there was another moment of perfection. How arbitrary they are, those moments. How transient.

As soon as I realized I could stay warm, negativity started to rise again. I think it began with wondering how I would spend my time now that I had found a perfect place in which to spend it. It wasn't even noon yet; I had the better part of a day ahead of me not worrying about survival, and what would I do? That's always a treacherous question for me: what shall I do? It presumes I should be doing something, which is a mistake to begin with. So it set off those awful doing-thoughts about myself again: how I'd failed at doing so many things, disappointed so many people. I tried to pray a little, tried to empty my mind, tried to think of myself being empty, tried to get comfortable in my little rocky cave space, tried to quit trying. The thoughts were beginning to wear me down: *I'm really no good, never have been. I'm a fake, a sorrowful charade of a person, God help me.* My perfect spot was becoming a prison of stone and snow, and I thought briefly, *I'll just split out of here, climb out and slide down the path and stumble back to the car and drive on home and have a couple of drinks and maybe things will be better tomorrow.*

But then the sun crisped itself through a break in the clouds, and though it was still snowing there were shafts of light, incredibly brilliant upon and within the trees, and my eyes were taken into the forest beneath me. A flutter of red and black off to the left, smacking up against a worm-eaten, storm-damaged tree. It was a pileated woodpecker, the kind you hear in the forest that sound like jackhammers. They're all big, but this one was huge, a crimson-capped monster who just sat there upright on the tree trunk being beautiful in the snow and the bright sun rays. *Why, I* wondered to the bird, *are you here at all? What grubs or beetles do you hope to find in that midwinter tree? What do you think you are doing?*

He only sat there, or perched there, or whatever they do when they've adhered themselves to the side of an old tree. Looking left and right, he just hung on the dead bark, being nothing but beautiful. The tree, I noticed, was wholly and completely dead. Not just winter-dead, winter-still like the other trees around, but finally and substantially dead, dead for years. Its limbs were gray and full of holes, its branches broken, its bark shredded and nearly gone, its trunk bald, decomposed. It was a corpse of a tree, and it would not turn green when spring came. It would never, ever be green again.

Yeah, I thought to the tree, *I know what it's like. Done your best and it wasn't good enough. Old and rotten to the core. Decaying, ugly.* But as soon as the thought passed, I realized the tree was not ugly at all. Its gray deadness bleached out against the snow and flecked against the darker black live trees and formed a counterpoint to the white-black-red of the bird and was . . . perfect. Then I looked where the woodpecker was looking, toward the south, and there were empty skeleton trees there, and evergreen pines, and when I looked at the trees as individuals I saw all the imperfections of them. Each was broken here and there; all had branches cracked by winds and ice, some split down the middle by lightning; many bore the scars of disease, blighted spots, knots and burls and parasite vines upon them, broken, wounded, growing this way and that, all with their injuries of the years and their imperfections of birth and growth and yet all were absolutely perfect as they were.

I thought, just a little, about perfection. I didn't become philosophical about it; it was just that I had seen, when I looked where the pileated woodpecker was looking, that perfection is just another sensation, determined by my mood, impermanent, transient, depending on my frame of mind. Every single one of these trees, however damaged and diseased and disfigured, was absolutely perfect in its own right in its own place there in the snow on the hillside. And I? It was quite natural, then, to see myself like a tree, imperfect in so many ways and yet, somehow, seen with the eyes of beauty, absolutely perfect. Oh, God, you woodpecker. You woodpecker God. You answered my prayer, you silly terrific whoever-you-are, you funny wonderful being at the heart of me and everything. I cannot help but love you, you know that.

The woodpecker flew away, to another dead crumbling tree as if to underscore his point, and I knew then that the woodpecker was God's being, like the trees and the children were God's being, like I am God's being, a sweetness of life.[11]

I sat gazing into the imperfect perfect trees until the sun moved beyond the hilltop above me and the cold penetrated my bones and even the hot chocolate that took nearly half an hour to get warm on my Sterno wouldn't warm me. It was time to go home. I pried myself out of the little cave and stretched my joints. It was the end of the day and I was soporific, floating in a sea of snow and coldness and the beauty of all imperfections, sliding along the trail in my cowboy boots.

About halfway back to the car I heard the sound of the children, laughing and shouting. They were coming down a side trail that joined mine right behind me. They were moving faster than I was—because they had sneakers in the snow and all I had was my cowboy boots—and once again I felt I had to elude them. I tried to run, fell, scrambled, stumbled, slipped, and scurried down the trail, keeping ahead of their laughing sounds. But this time it wasn't desperate; it was delightful. Toward the end of the trail, wheezing with my heart thumping like it wasn't going to beat much longer, I skidded one last time and slid down the whole last thirty feet of the hillside on my rump, laughing and hoping the little darlings couldn't see me being such a fool. No more thoughts of outdoor woodsman Jerry. I was just being there, running ahead of the kids and not caring too much, really, if they came up on me, and for all that I could have been a pileated woodpecker.

When I got back to the car, way ahead of the kids, panting and exhausted and feeling just wonderful in all my imperfection, I tossed my backpack and walking stick in through the little back window and climbed in and peeled off my boots and socks soaked with snowmelt. I put the key in the ignition and hauled back on the four-wheel-drive shift, and it was broken. The car wouldn't go into four-wheel drive, and so I couldn't feel so potent anymore, but the roads were clear enough and the two-wheel drive worked well enough and everything was perfect.

Eight

THE NAME OF
THE EAGLE

I went out seeking love,
and with unfaltering hope
I flew so high, so high,
that I overtook the prey.

—SAINT JOHN OF THE CROSS, *STANZAS GIVEN A SPIRITUAL MEANING*

The bird who guided me through my perfection lessons was *Dryo-copus pileatus*, a pileated woodpecker. That's what we have named him, for his bright red *pileus* ("cap") and his habit of pecking wood. According to the Book of Genesis, we can call him anything we want, for we human beings are the namers of all creation. I don't believe it for a minute, but Genesis says God gave us this power as a sign of our dominion over the earth and its creatures. If it wasn't obvious before, it is now: I don't believe in the inerrancy of Scripture. And in some cases, like this one, I believe in its errancy.[12]

I wonder how responsible those Genesis writers are for our current feeling of separation from Nature, with their notions of a transcendent God creating us out of the earth and then telling us to subjugate it. I suspect the delusion goes deeper than their writings, though, and that they were simply reinforcing a larger cultural animosity toward Nature. They were right about one thing, though: we are namers. We cannot help ourselves; we are compelled to name everything. Everything we encounter, every experience we have, every perception and feeling: we must call it by name. If we do not know the name, we create one. We cannot bear the nameless.

When faced with the nameless, we feel vulnerable, out of control. As physicians have always known, naming is reassuring. "What you have," says the doctor, "is idiopathic dysfunctionality." The diagnosis means something is wrong, but no one knows what it is, what caused it, or what can be done about it. Still, the patient is consoled. Even such a meaningless name gives at least the illusion of control. And when we are able to name a thing meaningfully, we feel a kind of power over it.

All too often, naming is truly a sign of subjugation. Masters name their slaves; owners name their pets; bigots name their enemies; angry children call each other names. To name in this way is to try to possess, conquer, or control. There are, of course, many ways of naming that convey respect and even reverence, but these are also acts of power; they are always the choice of the namer. A still more respectful way is not to give a name but to discover it. But even learning a being's true name is to claim some of its power, to grasp something of its soul.

On a summer Sunday morning in the place of fields and meadows, long after I had tried to draw the great matriarch tree against the sunrises, I returned and sat beneath her intricate branches. This time I had brought along my field guide to American trees. I tried to find her species, but identifying her was as difficult as drawing her had been. The smooth oblong shape of her alternate leaves, her deep rough bark, and her huge size fit no description in my book. I gave up that day, aware of a subtle uneasiness.

Later I asked a friend for help in identifying the tree, and I consulted other books. Finally I found it: black tupelo, blackgum, sourgum, *Nyssa sylvatica*. That's what the tree had to be; everything fit except for the tree's giant size; she is simply an unusually large specimen. I stood beneath her then, knowing her name, and felt a gaping painful distance between myself and the tree. Something had changed, something had been lost, something was wounded. I felt sorrow, and I sensed she had somehow done her best to resist the naming in the same way I believed she moved her branches when no one was looking. She must have known what the naming would do.

FRANKLIN TREES

Plants and other creatures are often named in honor of their discoverers or of other dignitaries. The creature, without being asked, becomes forever dedicated to the one for whom it is named. So it was with the ladybug, named in the Middle Ages for the mother of Jesus. Such was also the case of the Franklin tree,

Franklinia alatamaha, named for Benjamin Franklin by the Philadelphia botanist who discovered it.[13]

Years ago, when they dammed the river to form the reservoir near my home, the northernmost waters flooded over the remains of an abandoned mill town. On rare occasions, when the water level is very low, you can still see the submerged walls of buildings where people once lived and worked. The old road to the village still exists, now running directly into the water as a boat launch. A hundred yards west of the launch is a tiny stream, coming from a spring that once provided drinking water for the townspeople. It was along this stream that I first encountered the Franklin trees.

You'd probably not notice Franklin trees in winter and spring, but in late summer and early fall when other trees are thinking about retiring, these erupt in a profusion of blooms. Their blossoms are like miniature magnolias, with soft white-pink shells of beauty that open and then fall upon the grass and upon the asphalt of the parking lot that has been built there. When you come close to them on an early September morning when the air is still, their fragrance sweeps you into itself. It is not an aroma to be sniffed and commented upon; it simply absorbs you and makes you beautiful.

The blossoms are very delicate; you can pick one up from the ground and it will open itself to you as you turn it in your hands. The texture is so creamy you almost have to touch the petals to your cheek, slide them across your lips. It is the most sensual flower I have ever known. Near the trees stand two carved signs. One commemorates the submerged mill town and the still-flowing spring; the other announces that this species of trees is one of the "rarest ornamentals" in the country, and that they were named in honor of Benjamin Franklin. I know no more about the trees, but I do know something about Benjamin Franklin. I know he was a great inventor, writer, and statesman. I know his attitude toward Native Americans and the wilderness was malignant. I also know he wanted the national bird of the United States to be the turkey.

TURKEYS

Some creatures are named for their place of origin, like African elephants and Canada geese. This can be a respectful way of naming—if we get it right. As Benjamin Franklin knew, the turkey is a completely American bird, but for some reason the original namer of the turkey thought it came from the country of Turkey.

The association with the country is now long forgotten, and the name *turkey* has become synonymous with silliness and stupidity. Except for its association with a fine brand of bourbon, the turkey has become a joke of a bird in the national psyche. This is not the fault of the naming but of our actual subjugation of the animal. We have completely bred away all wildness and cunning in domesticated turkeys, the ones raised for dinners, so they are indeed silly and stupid. Occasionally you read about them escaping, running flapping and gobbling through a town and the citizens chase them and the whole adventure is hilarious.

But once on the forested mountain I glimpsed wild turkeys moving gently through the underbrush. There were three of them I think, a male and two hens, but I am not certain. Nor do I know how long they had been there, utterly silent, before my eyes sensed a hint of their movement. They appeared much like the domesticated breed, yet darker, the male's wattle dusky red, subdued. They moved with such silent steadiness and grace that they seemed almost to flow through brush and branches. I reached for my camera and they were gone. No flurry, no rush, no evidence of panic, not even a sound. They had simply disappeared. Afterward, there was one word in my mind: dignity.

But it is still the pitiful, stupid, domesticated food-bird that the name *turkey* brings to mind for most people. As the saying goes, "It's hard to soar like an eagle when you're working with turkeys." Most people in the United States are very grateful to have the bald eagle instead of the turkey as their national symbol. As I understand it, the name of the eagle has very simple origins; its roots go back to *aqua*, the Latin word for water. Many eagles, including the species that became the national symbol, make their homes along watersides.

Perhaps such simple naming allows us to appreciate a creature more for what it truly is. Whatever the reason, the majesty of an eagle soaring through the sky transcends all naming. It is not surprising that the eagle has become such a symbol of dignity, such an archetype of freedom. To be sure, we have damaged eagles in many ways: hunting them for feathers, destroying their habitats, allowing pesticides to soften their eggs, for a while almost driving even the bald eagles to extinction. But we have not impugned their dignity by naming. And, thank God, we have not domesticated them.

I have encountered four eagles in the wild: two golden eagles at a distance, two bald eagles close up. I much preferred the golden eagles at a distance, so I will tell that story first.

GOLDEN EAGLES

It is the third day of my week-long solitude retreat in the Jemez Mountains of New Mexico in the summer of 1993. I am sitting on the deck of a small cabin and I am well into the silence, absorbed by the majesty of the mesas to the east and west, my awareness swallowed into limitless vistas of desert where the canyon opens in the south. As I so often do when it is totally unnecessary, I am trying to meditate. Why, when everything around me is perfect and I am immersed in the moment, do I still think I must *do* something to be contemplative? It is always only by a gift that I am allowed to just be. Left to my own devices, I will always be trying to do something—even if what I am trying to do is nothing.

Nothing is what I am trying to do as the morning sunlight flows down the side of the western mesa. I sit cross-legged on a Navajo rug, back straight, breathing in the high-desert air that is like wakefulness itself. My eyes are slightly open, seeing but not really looking at the endless desert. A soft silent prayer arises, *I am yours.* There is stillness all around, but I know I'm trying too hard, working at something, holding something somewhere. I try to relax everything, surrender myself completely, but that too is trying. Then I hear the eagle's call. I do not know it as eagle yet, but it is a cry that pierces me once, twice, a third time, going directly into my heart, into the very center of my longing. It is as if that center of me had suddenly shrieked out of itself, crying into the empty mountain air, echoing back and forth between the high mesa walls. My head turns to the sound and there I see two slowly moving forms above the mesa, black against the utterly clean blue sky, high above the great red-white rocks and windblown piñon trees.

The cry comes again through the air to me, more into my heart than my ears. I reach for my binoculars and focus on one of the birds. It is brown, not black, a burnished russet soaring, and the cry comes once more and it is more wild, more empty than anything I have ever known. The cry seems to me to be utterly without emotion yet somehow made of pure yearning. How can something so free of feeling be so totally passionate? It is a cry of the absolute, a stark scream of truth, completely and purely wild in the height, in the flight, in the all-consuming sky. I follow the bird's movement through the binoculars. It handles the thin air, the mountain breeze flawlessly. There is neither mastery nor defeat, just the simple piercing perfection of utterly straight wings and clean air, and the sharp cry of being alive.

I want so desperately to cry that way myself, to shriek out my own truth into the endless emptiness, to shout out my longing, my nameless passion in the same simple, totally complete way. I want my soul-sound to fly out against the mesa walls like that bird's cry, but it is unutterable for me, caught within the walls of my chest, inexpressible. Something distinctly human in me, something civilized, keeps my cry inside. And then the eagle cries again, and I think—in the manner of thinking that is without thoughts really forming—that the great bird is crying for me. Not crying in sympathy with me or compassion for me, but crying in my stead because I cannot. In this moment, the eagle's call is an intercession for me, a standing-in-my-place, an expression of my simple aliveness made possible in a freedom that I do not possess, in eagle freedom. I know why this is a holy bird, a sacred creature, for I suddenly feel an earth-deep *need* for this eagle to cry out my soul, to sing my utmost prayer in the heights of emptiness. My prayer then becomes suddenly real, very intimate, very direct, and it is a prayer of gratitude for the eagle who sings my prayer.

BALD EAGLES

I had encountered the bald eagles a year earlier, on the reservoir a few miles south of where the Franklin trees grow. The canoe was new to me then and I was just becoming comfortable with her. She and I and the wind were beginning to understand one another. I was exploring coves, little stream inlets that feed the big water. The banks of these coves hold treasures of driftwood, shells, beaver-felled trees, rich sweet growth in the early summer, and way back in the shallows of their very beginnings you may discover a tiny waterfall. I was in a particularly long, winding cove, paddling softly close to the shoreline, going deeper and deeper toward the hidden stream-source. I was listening carefully for waterfall sounds. I was expectant.

I heard no waterfall, no sound at all except that of a distant woodpecker as I approached the stream that fed the cove. The water spread wider there, into a shallow marsh, and I had to navigate around floating logs and submerged stumps. I could glimpse the stream entrance, hidden behind an overgrowth of shrubs and tall marsh grasses and arching trees. Intent upon my gentle navigation toward that hidden source, I suddenly felt fear.

What followed took only a few seconds, but my memory plays it back frame by frame in painfully slow, unforgivingly complete detail. I am certain my first sensation was fear. Perhaps I had heard a rustling of great feathers upon the air, or maybe I had caught a subtle glimpse of movement, a reflection in the water, but all I recall is fear of a great unfriendly presence, approaching me, coming very fast. The fear-feeling in my chest forced my eyes upward, to the tree line and the sky and there, silent and absolutely huge, with a wingspan wider than I am tall, the great bird came straight at me, dead on course.

We all have our own repertoires of fear, colored by our peculiar history of terrible experiences. There wasn't time to recognize it then, but what I felt was something left from Vietnam—the scrambling hopeless terror of vulnerable human flesh in the path of huge war machines: tanks, rockets, jet fighters carrying napalm. The eagle was in a shallow dive, soundless and at immense speed directly in line with my canoe in exactly the way a fighter plane is over you before you hear it. I think I understand, just a little, what a rabbit or mouse feels just before being hit by a predator bird.

The sun is blotted out for an instant by something of vast vicious power and there's no time to get away and you somehow know it but you try anyway, or at least you just begin to try, and then it is all over. I became fear in that instant, pure embodied terror. It was the size of the thing, the sheer size.

I managed one jerking paddle-stroke, enough to angle the canoe slightly away from the eagle's course. At what seemed the final moment of my existence, the eagle leveled off at less than fifteen feet above my head. On course straight-and-true, just like a fighter dropping its load of napalm, the eagle dropped its load. Like napalm canisters, a series of globs and blobs smashed into the water exactly where my canoe had been an instant before, laid out in a pattern almost precisely sixteen feet long, the length of the canoe. Eagle shit. The bird tried to shit on me. The splash where it hit the water went at least two feet into the air and sprayed into the canoe.

It is very difficult to describe the mixture of feelings I experienced. I was awestruck, and though a slight hilarity wanted to rise in me, it could not break through the pervading terror I still felt. Just as I had been overwhelmed by the sheer size of the bird, I was aghast at the sheer amount of fecal material it had released. Tiny thoughts started to form. *My God, how could you be so full of . . . , That bird has got to be sick . . . , Do eagles actually do that?* I was still all adrenaline and absolutely convinced that if the shit had hit me directly I would have died. Unwisely, my jaw was hanging open.

After its attack run, the eagle sailed directly into a tree where it sat motionless, still completely silent, coldly watching me. As if in response to some unuttered question, it slightly twitched its tail and shit again. "All right!" I shouted, "I'm leaving! I'm outta here!" I truly had no desire to remain. I was completely committed to leaving the cove, leaving the whole place to the eagle. I no longer cared about waterfalls or stream sources. I simply wanted to live.

I turned the canoe around with three good strokes and was just beginning to pick up speed when another eagle, the mate I assume, suddenly appeared from the same direction as the first, diving toward me with the same deadly perfection. It is one thing to be attacked in total surprise, and quite another to be attacked when you've already acknowledged defeat and are in full retreat. This time, my terror was frosted with humiliation.

I felt completely beaten when I saw the second eagle diving. I had no reflexes left with which to alter the canoe's course. I simply sat and watched it come. I cannot say I was calm, but there was a kind of stillness in me, the simplicity of accepting something wholly inevitable. This too, I imagine, is something rabbits and mice sometimes experience. And perhaps little children, sometimes.

It's hard for me to believe the eagle sensed my defeat, but for some reason it changed course slightly, toward the front of the canoe. It crossed ahead of me, laying another sixteen-foot pattern of shit at a perfect right angle to the canoe. A shot across my bow. The bird sailed on into the tree, coming to rest on a dead branch above its mate. I paddled slowly out of the cove, out of the place that was so clearly theirs. I looked back at them once before I rounded a point. They were completely motionless, looking away from me, back toward the trees from which they had attacked. There, I assume, was their nest.

I've told the story many times, and it always comes out funny. But there is more to it for me. When I tell it, I can never seem to communicate how complete was my terror, or how abject my surrender. I can't convince my friends that I really believed the shit would kill me. They try to understand, they really want to, but they can't stop laughing and I get to laughing too, and it all becomes impossible to take seriously, which in the long run is probably just as well.

Occasionally some of those friends asked me to take them where the eagles tried to shit on me, and I did go back there, tentatively, several times. I never saw those two eagles again. I hoped they were all right, and that bald eagles do sometimes defend their territories by shitting on invaders. I've read that howler monkeys do it. They'll run through the tree branches to the perimeters of their territory and dump right square on anyone or anything that tries to enter. I understand it's a very effective defense. So maybe eagles do it too.

In subsequent years, I solicited comments from a number of raptor authorities about this kind of behavior in predator birds. One recounted a similar experience with an owl but said, "I don't think it was intentional." Another, more recently, said it is indeed common behavior for bald eagles, especially when they have chicks in their nest.

So I hope the eagles weren't sick. I hope they did have a nest in that cove, and that there were healthy little baby eagles in there, and that those babies have now grown up strong and have had chicks of their own who can, if need be, shit on somebody else.

Nine
RAINSTORMS

Oh, clouds, rain down from your height,
earth needs you . . .

—SAINT JOHN OF THE CROSS, *ROMANCES*

I remember lying on my back as a child, making what I wanted out of cloud shapes, those most ancient and gentle of Rorschachs. I still do it occasionally, but now I tend to tire more quickly of making something of anything, and often I just rest and let the clouds and the sky that holds them be what they are, let myself be who I am. Then sometimes it seems the sky takes me into itself—or rather reveals that I am already and always inside it, for the sky does eternally embrace everything. It holds the earth and all creatures within itself. I am always healed in such moments.

Sooner or later, I suspect, the sky could teach us everything. It is willing for that. It waits to be noticed, to be looked into. The apostle Paul is supposed to have said we live and move and have our being in God. If that's true, one might ask, how come God often seems so far away? Maybe it's something like the sky. The sky often seems distant, but it's always embracing us; it always has and always will. It not only holds us; it flows through us. We breathe it. It's in our blood, in every cell. And always we are soaring through its endless reaches, and forever we are a part of it and it a part of us. I can almost feel the sky waiting to be noticed, wanting to be appreciated, loving to be wondered at. It forms thousands of events to get our attention. It manifests a cloud right around us and we say "it's foggy." It showers us and we say "it's raining." And it storms.

THUNDER AND LIGHTNING

I hadn't noticed it before I went to the mountain alone, but rainstorms are like people. Each rainstorm has a personality, and no two are exactly alike. Perhaps I had sensed this as a little boy and simply forgotten. I recall sitting on the big porch swing with my grandmother, watching a storm come in over the fields, and she'd talk to me about it and she'd have her arm around me and the worn fabric of her dress and the thin wisps of her gray hair would flutter in the freshening breeze. She was probably trying to keep me from being afraid of the thunder and lightning, but she must have had some appreciation of storm personalities. "Ah, just watch this," she'd say. "This is gonna be a nice one."

She told me that thunder was the sound of giants rolling barrels around in the sky. My mother told me it was God's stomach growling, and I wondered who was right. I preferred giants and barrels. My grandmother taught me how you can smell a storm coming, or at least smell the rain long before it begins, in the same way that you can sniff the presence of the ocean long before you get there.

And it was she who comforted me through a Florida hurricane when everything turned dark and the wind blew a huge bird against the side of the house and killed it and took most of its feathers away and stirred the water moccasins out of the lake and roared with the loudest, longest, most ominously powerful sound I had ever heard. "Just a big rain," she told me then. "It's just a big rain."

Both my mother and my grandmother spent considerable effort making sure I wasn't afraid of thunder and lightning. They had both grown up on farms, and I guess they knew that children and animals are easily frightened by thunder, and getting things done on the farm meant you couldn't be cowering someplace every time a storm came up. So they filled my head with images of giant barrels and cosmic stomachs so I wouldn't be afraid. But I could sense they themselves were afraid, at least a little. When an adult keeps telling you there's nothing to be afraid of, you know there probably is.

In my family there were stories of people who had been killed in the fields by lightning, and of at least one farm completely lost to a "cyclone." And there was the often-repeated tale of old great-uncle Sanford who, as he got on in years, would sit on his farmhouse porch and do nothing but wait for thunderstorms to come. On a likely summer afternoon he would sit there in the heat for hours, glaring at the sky, waiting. When the storm finally came, and when the thunder and lightning began, he would haul up out of his chair and run out in the open field behind the barn and stand, legs apart, feet planted firmly in the soybeans, fist shaking at the sky, and he would scream into the clouds, "Strike down old Sanford if ya dare!"

I never saw him do it; I only heard the stories. I have just the vaguest memory of old Sanford, sitting, glaring and daring, on his porch. I remember he was a scary guy, much more frightening than thunder and lightning. It was the look on his face, his clear readiness to tackle any insult, any affront. Deep inside himself, Sanford was on patrol. His eyes were ready, defiant, and dangerous.

As I reflect on it, there were a lot of scary people in my mother's family of Scots-Irish farmers. I think it had something to do with their always feeling affronted by Nature. They were of the European stock that carried in their bones a basic animosity toward wildness. The land was to be tamed, the animals to be domesticated or hunted, and the weather—it just had to be coped with. Although they were now mostly Methodists, they had inherited a penetrating Presbyterian hopelessness about never really winning. You might clear the fields and plow the land and eradicate most of the varmints, but the weather could—and eventually would—get you. So I guess old Sanford was a family archetype, in his feeble years embodying the rage of a people who had set themselves against Nature, knowing they'd never win. The family chuckled about old Sanford behind his back, but I think they rather liked it when he shook his fist against the sky. To my knowledge, nobody ever tried to stop him.

For the most part, my mother taught me that I should defend myself against Nature. In winter she bundled me against the cold, and at any sign of rain she outfitted me with raincoat and galoshes, and sometimes even an umbrella. It was "bad weather" when it rained, a "nice day" when it didn't. Somewhere in my adolescence my friends and I entertained the question, When you're caught in the rain and you run to get out of it, do you get wetter because you're running into more drops, or do you stay drier because you get out of the rain faster? I guess we all shared the idea that it's somehow not good to get wet in the rain. I'm not sure why. Little kids and lovers like it well enough.

About the only characteristics I gave to rainstorms in my childhood were "nice" and "hard." Nice rain was the gentle kind that you could hear soothingly on a roof or a car top or on a tent at night. Hard rain meant a storm and a little electrified anxiety, a hint of dangerous possibilities. Much later I learned that some Native Americans in the Southwest call these female and male rains; female rain is soft and steady enough to soak in and water the ground; male rain runs off the surface and sometimes makes flash floods.

TENT RAIN

The second time I went alone to the mountain was in the late summer of 1990, in the season of afternoon thunderstorms. I had read in my Boy Scout Handbook that if you use a little care in placing your tent and ground cloth, you don't have to insult the earth by digging those old-fashioned trenches around your campsite to carry off water. So I followed the advice: tent on a level spot, ground cloth folded under the tent's edges. I was prepared for rain if it should come. The first afternoon, as I was drowsing hot and languid under a tree, I noticed a stillness come over the forest. The birds and cicadas, who had been providing a steady background sound, fell quiet. The air seemed heavier, expectant. I knew it meant rain coming; these were signs I had experienced all my life but had never really been conscious of before.

I walked to a clearing where I could look off to the southwest, and there a soft, dark, almost tentative cloudiness was arising. Slowly the breeze came, brushing around the trees and cooling little parts of me, as if it were scouting ahead, seeking some kind of welcome. I checked my tent, covered what might blow away, and then just stood there in the clearing. Overhead, white baby cumulus puff clouds still sailed through brilliant blue background sky, but the distant darkness along the mountainside was growing closer, feeling its way, and lightning brightened it. Soft rumbles of thunder came.

Standing there just looking, feeling the undecided breeze on my skin and hearing it rustle the trees, smelling its freshness, I had the sense that this particular rainstorm wasn't going to come all the way to me. It was too uncertain, too delicate, not fully gathered on its course. Without a reason, I found myself wishing a little power into the clouds, wanting more strength for them, hoping the storm would grow into maturity. But as I expected, the breeze lessened and the darkness in the distance became translucent, then misty, and then was gone. The faintest huff of thunder faded into a brief silence before the birds and insects began to sing again. It was almost sad, to stand and watch a storm not quite happen. It had only a slight beginning, and then it was no more, like an infant thought rising in consciousness, never taking shape, just a little bit of energy appearing for a while, then disappearing, leaving not so much as a memory.

It was hot the rest of the afternoon and through the night. Few breezes moved, and heavy humid air hovered on the mountainside, blanketing the trees and everything within, closer than intimacy, too close. The next afternoon, at about the same time, the scene repeated itself. I was drowsing again under the same tree when the animal sounds stopped. Walking to the clearing, I saw another storm. This one had a completely different personality. High, white, fully formed thunderheads foamed over the mountainside, dark rain pouring beneath them. This was a dreadnought of a rainstorm. I knew this one was coming all the way and nothing on earth would change it. When the breeze came it was already a wind, sure of its direction, uncaring, unwavering, and almost before I felt it I heard leaves crisply severed from their branches, and the crackle of the branches themselves. The air chilled against my skin, drying the sweat and grime of the last hot night and day on me, and the atmosphere around me felt merciless, almost fierce. This oncoming storm made me want to stand tall, to be like a tree as it approached. This was a storm that needed no encouragement, a storm completely unconcerned with welcome. Perhaps the genes I inherited from old Sanford had awakened, for I felt I somehow needed to meet this storm face-to-face.

I had laid a fire, a big fire ready to be lit for the evening, but something about the wind made me want to light it now, to have it burning strong when the storm came. I knelt in the ashes at the fire pit, striking several matches that the wind extinguished. I had to turn my back to the oncoming storm and light the kindling under my bent body, and then the wind fanned the fire, and the fire grew and made a new wind-sound, a burning sound against the blowing brushing leaves and branches. The flames were high when I heard the first thunder, and the fire was going very strong when the first huge drops of rain fell upon the fire and me. I stood downwind of the fire, at first to guard against blowing sparks, but then for the warmth of it as the rain and wind covered my skin.

I stood very much like a tree there on the northeast side of the fire, feeling its heat glow on my body, hearing the sizzle of raindrops falling on the coals, breathing in the smoke of it, and the rain-fresh air. The combined cold of the rain on me and heat of the fire on me, both made penetrating by the wind, created a sensation unlike anything I had ever felt. I savored the feeling, reveled in it, found it delicious and thought that if a hot fudge sundae had feelings, it must feel like this.

The rain came fully then, pouring down upon the fire and turning into billowing windblown steam, rivering over my skin, bathing me, freshening me. I shivered with the coldness of the rain and moved closer to the fire-steam. The heat drove me back into the rain chill, and then, cold again, I hopped back toward the fire, and I was dancing. To dance with no idea of dancing, to swirl and leap in the breeze and sizzling fire with no thought of how or when to move, how wonderful! I danced and danced in the ashes-turning-into-mud, and sounds came from me that were howls of simple delight and moans of primitive longing and grunts of pure sexuality and none of it contrived and all of it some kind of prayer. One thought, just once, about how blessed I was to have no one else around and to be free to be so wildly wedded to the storm and fire.

Thunder came and it was my song, and the wind my courtesan, and praise welled up inside me as the rain poured, drenching down around and in and through me until the fire finally died under its flow and there was nothing but cold dark chilling water covering everything, running down my legs into rivulets into streams and puddles, too fast to soak into the earth, just running, streaming in darkness and the thunder moved off to the north and the wind steadied and the rain just came. Stillness entered me with the chill, my chest heaving, and my belly clenching in the cold. I stuck my head into the tent, grabbed a towel and dried my hair and face, turned around and dried my back and bottom with my legs still sticking out in the rain, and then dried one leg at a time, slowly backing into the tent like a hermit crab being very casual. I crawled into my sleeping bag and just lay there, listening to the storm move on, off, away to the north, and the rain still coming down, and it was pretty much heaven.

Sometime later, as the rain dwindled to a drizzle, I thought how sad it is that all these rainstorms come and go and I so seldom really notice them. In my home and office I may be vaguely aware that it's raining, but a thunderstorm has to be very severe before it really gets my attention—and then most often it's only an aggravation. I don't feel the power of the storms, don't sense their fierceness, and never, ever dance. And I miss entirely those delicate little storms that never quite make it to the big time. How many are there, I wondered, that die before being noticed by anyone? I felt like apologizing for missing the personalities of the storms, and I thought about making some resolve to notice the sky and weather more, but I knew it wouldn't be authentic. Resolutions seldom are.

CABIN RAIN

In the summer of 1993, riding through the New Mexico desert to the cabin where I saw the golden eagles, I followed the Rio Grande north from Albuquerque and then up Route 4 along the Jemez River into the San Diego Canyon. In the open lands before entering the canyon, New Mexico has endless sky. I could see rainstorms coming from miles and miles away. Even within the canyon, I could watch the storms pass far to the south or north, crowned with thunderheads, trailing sheets of gray rainfall beneath them. At such distances their moving seems stately, a formal procession of weather-beings. From the cabin itself, set high between the canyon walls, I could be watching a storm far to the south when suddenly, without warning, another would sneak in from the west over the rim of Virgin Mesa and be upon me before I knew it. Then, wind and rain would come at once, with no stateliness whatsoever, and in the rainy season it could be merciless.

One afternoon I walked about five miles through the mountains into town to pick up provisions. I had tried it once before on my first day there and had only made it back because an Indian jewelry trader had given me a lift partway in his van. Then I had been very out of shape, my muscles not used to the mountain terrain, my heart still unaccustomed to the altitude. My knees and hips had started to lock up, and the man in the van had been a savior. But this second time I felt more fit; I was certain I could make it if I paced myself. I had filled my backpack at the little store and stopped at the saloon for a burger and green chili and a couple of beers. It was late afternoon when I started back, at least three hours before dark. I was tired, but I knew I'd make it.

About halfway down the road it began to rain. Gentle drops, cooling me, giving vigor and spirit as I walked. No problem if I get soaked, I thought, for the temperature was still high. Even so, I was getting tired and I still had a mile and a half to go, the last five hundred feet of which were almost straight up the side of the mesa. I was walking on the left side of the road, against the sparse oncoming traffic, when a white pickup passed me from behind, went over a rise, then came back on my side of the road and stopped next to me. The young driver, a construction worker, asked if he could give me a ride. "You sure can," I said. "You'll save my feet from wearing out and the rest of me from getting soaked."

We spoke little—both of us listening to the rhythm of the windshield wipers because that was the sound that was there—

but when he dropped me at the foot of my little side canyon I meant it when I said, "Much obliged." As I trudged up the last five hundred feet I began to wonder about my earlier confidence. Would I have made it without the ride? It was a minor question, only curiosity, until I got to the cabin almost completely winded and put the key in the door. At that very instant a storm came over the western mesa, a killer storm, a mountain-lion storm, leaping upon the valley, its unsuspecting prey.

In its power the rain did not simply fall but was catapulted horizontally by winds that bent the piñon trees and uprooted prickly pears and sent them scurrying across the sand into rocky crevasses. Hail the size of marbles flew nearly parallel to the ground, crashing and ricocheting like musket balls against the boulders, and I could see flash floods churning down half a dozen arroyos and pouring across the road where I had been walking. I was safely inside by then, but I wondered quietly what I would have done if the young man in the pickup had not come back to get me, if I had been caught out in that predator storm. With strange calmness it occurred to me that I truly might have died. There was no shelter save that of caves made by huge boulders precariously perched on top of one another, boulders that shifted and tumbled in the flood. I felt cared for then, as if I must have been worth preserving, and I smiled, and then I slept, embraced by blankets, by the cabin's soft brown wood, and by the starless, howling sky.

Ten

NATURAL BEING

I will head for the mountains and for watersides;
I will not gather flowers, nor fear wild beasts . . .
—SAINT JOHN OF THE CROSS, *SPIRITUAL CANTICLE*

That night, in the cabin, as I slept through the rainstorm, I had a dream about a mountain lion. In the dream I walked out the back door of my house and there was a high wooden fence around the yard and the mountain lion was crouched on top of the fence. Children from another yard were yelling and throwing rocks at him. His great gray body was utterly still except for his long soft tail swaying slightly and his head turning left and right, slowly, simply looking. He looked at the children and then back toward me, his eyes passing over me completely open, seeing me and everything around me and I was nothing special to him. I sensed no expression on his face, no emotion in his deep eyes, only complete perceptiveness, cat-being. A stone bounced off his haunch and I could see a slight twitch of muscle there beneath the smooth fur. In the dream, I knew he would move soon; I knew he would not abide the harassment much longer. But he seemed unperturbed, completely calm.

I sensed from the movements of his head that he was in no way cornered. His options were wide open. He could attack the children; he could be upon them in one bound. He could leap toward me. He could do anything he wanted from his perch on the fence. I was frightened by his power and his vast possibility, but I was also fascinated by his stillness, how he took his time. I thought he must be deciding what to do, but I knew immediately that decision making was not happening inside him. What was happening inside him could not be known to me.

He stood. He was huge. In one smooth movement he leaped from the fence toward me, over my head like a gray brushstroke on the sky to the top of another fence behind me and to my left. Tail straight behind him, not looking back, he walked to the end of the fence, jumped down on the grass, crossed the street, and started up a hill toward an old barn. In my dream I followed him. Compared to his movements, mine seemed erratic, undefined, tentative. He seemed so certain, so sure of himself. Yet I also knew that certainty and self-assurance were not in him. It was something deeper and cleaner, something less complicated and much more powerful.

I was far behind him when he reached the barn. I saw him go up some steps and disappear inside. I struggled up the hill and peeked through the door. Inside, the building appeared to be a rodeo arena. No people were there, but there were horses in a central corral and they were very afraid, whinnying and running back and forth. High above them the mountain lion was leaping, gliding in graceful arcs from rafter to rafter. In my dream-knowing I was sure he had no hostile intent toward the horses. He was, in his own mountain lion way, playing.

Alighting on one beam, he suddenly stopped and turned and looked straight at me. His face was expressionless, but I sensed something in him that, finally, I knew and could understand. It was his enjoyment of the play, his body-pleasure in bounding through the air above the horses, and his pure sense-delight in their reaction to him, their sound and movement beneath him. I wanted to be just like him then, to feel what it was to be those muscles inside that great gray fur and to leap from rafter to rafter above the horses and to simply know what to do, to know so surely what comes next with not a single thought of it . . . but no, once again I'd lost touch with him. He doesn't know what comes next. It's more like he waits, is always waiting and watching and sniffing and listening, waiting for what *comes* next.

My dream thoughts had taken me somewhere, and when my gaze returned to the mountain lion his teeth were bared, his eyes fierce, and he was no longer playing. He leaped toward me from the beam, high over the horses. His great paws puffed the straw and the dry dirt of the floor where he landed, and he came for me. There was no decision making in me then, nor any self-assurance as I turned and ran toward the door. Yet I ran straight and clean and fast, and I could smell him and feel his presence closing behind me. To my right were four planks of barn siding laid across two high packing crates and I jumped up there and stood still. The lion, I knew, could easily have jumped up after me, but instead he stopped beside the crates and just looked up at me. Strange, I thought, that neither he nor I is out of breath. He looked up at me and I looked down at him, and it lasted quite a while. Then he turned and went out the door.

I awoke then, and lay for a long time in the blankets in the little brown cabin, my eyes closed. The dream had left a feeling in me, something of animal being, indescribable but sure, delicate in my mind but certain in my heart. I opened my eyes to the bright New Mexico morning. The storm had passed in the night.

ANIMAL BEING

Now, a dozen years later, the dream of the mountain lion remains fresh and clear in my mind. I wrote it in my journal, but there really was no need to. It is imprinted in my consciousness, and it continues to teach me.

At first I thought the teaching was about animal being, the mystery of what goes on inside the consciousness of wild creatures. Now, however, I believe the teaching of my dream—and the teaching that all wild things continually offer us—is really about ourselves, about human nature. I will never understand the inner life of a mountain lion, nor of any other animal. But I am sure that wild creatures share this one characteristic: they are completely, totally themselves. They do not pretend to be anything else. They do not question their identity. They do not second-guess themselves. They are what they are, and they are impeccable at it. They have no use for questions about their worth on earth. They *are* worthy.

Once I saw a stag in Rock Creek Park in the heart of the District of Columbia, an animal used to seeing people and allowing them to see him. He was slightly streetwise but wild enough, untamed. He nipped at branches and nibbled at grass, but frequently he stopped and stood very still for a long time. In these extended stillnesses he was smelling the air, listening to the sounds, looking, *seeing* all around. I sensed his feeling the ground beneath his hooves, feeling the sensations inside his strong, good body. He was impeccable.

The stag communicated a very dynamic, lively being-who-one-is-where-one-is. This is possible for us as well, if we can find our natural living wildness that actively feels itself and sniffs the air, sees everything clearly and listens with alert ears.

Do not think that deer—or human beings who have learned the lesson—become vigilant only to detect danger. The alertness is also to detect goodness: food, companionship, soft places, water, sunlight, shade, and sky. And more than that, it is to be appreciatively alive and responsive to where you are and what you will do next. The alertness goes inside as well as outside; it senses the quality of your heartbeat, the depth of your breath, the warmth of your hide, the comfort or tightness of your guts. It is feeling all your being in the completeness of your situation.

To do this well, the deer teaches, you must take many times to stand very still in the midst of whatever you are doing. Whether you are grazing or walking, running through the forest or drinking from a stream, you must stop and become very attentive. Lift your head; look and see what is around you. Perk your ears; listen and hear. Sniff the air. Feel your body. Move only that which helps you sense: shake your head a little, paw the ground a bit, take one breath that is deeper than most. Turn your head to look here or there, lick your tongue to taste your face. The stillness inside must become exquisite; it must deepen into a moment of absolutely pure and utterly simple wakefulness in which your whole being is vitally present. In this stillness, you exist in beauty, and your next movement is perfectly clear. It is the practical, immediate ground of both appreciation and wisdom.

Now, when I walk in the woods and fields, I like to stop, sometimes suddenly, sometimes softly. I stand like a tree. I look around and feel my body. I notice my breath steaming in the cool air. I sense inside, my emotions and heart-perceptions. My listening is sharp and my seeing acute. I feel the temperature, the sun or the snowflakes, and what thoughts or images may come to the surface of my mind. If I want to know which way to turn next, I wait, see, listen. My being lives and Wisdom comes.[14]

At the time I wrote those words, I wanted to be like the stag. And for a long time after my dream, I wanted to be exactly like the mountain lion: present, clear, free, and dead-sure. But in the dream, when he turned and chased me and I ran fast and straight, and when I leaped upon the packing crates without a thought and without missing a step, I was not being a mountain lion. I was being *me*, fully, immediately, wildly me.

The poet Rilke said, "Everything in Nature grows and defends itself in its own way and is characteristically and spontaneously itself, seeking at all costs to be so against all opposition."[15]

The attack of the mountain lion made me completely myself within the dream, and I have been more fully myself ever since. This, I am convinced, is the real teaching of wild creatures: by so fully being who they are, they show us how to be who we really are. This is the great lesson of the Wisdom of the wild.

HEALING

As I have said many times, Nature's teaching is also a healing. And although we must indeed be taught, it is the healing that we need most. We have been fractured. We have been broken off from the nature of our world, broken away from the nature of one another, broken apart from our own nature. The pain of this breach is so constant that we have become accustomed to it; it feels normal. The pain is with us every day, when we browbeat ourselves for not handling things right, when we judge ourselves and others, when we struggle for control, when we draw circles around ourselves that shut others out, when we long for a connectedness we cannot find, when we try to help one another and it's never enough, and, perhaps most of all, when we go outdoors and feel that Nature is something different from us.

You and I and every other human being on earth are part of Nature. Like it or not, our buildings, roads, billboards, and junk-yards are part of Nature. The smoke from our factories and the waste from our refineries are part of Nature. And all the things we do to try to protect the environment and save endangered species: these too are part of Nature. But no matter how kindly we feel, we will never be able to participate in healing the world around us as long as we keep seeing Nature as something different from ourselves.

Some of us still see the earth as an enemy, something to conquer, subjugate, and squander. More of us, thank God, now see it as something to cherish and to care for. But even in our cherishing, the earth remains an "it," a "something," an object that is not us. The popular language is "stewardship of the environment." Stewards are managers, overseers, caretakers, and no matter how benevolent they are, they must forever remain apart from that which they care for. We do not know who we really are in this world, and like zeal-blinded missionaries trying to help what they consider to be a primitive tribe, our well-meaning hands become abusive.

Before we can effectively heal the wounds we have inflicted upon the rest of Nature, we must allow ourselves to be healed. And we must allow the rest of Nature to help us. I do not know exactly how the healing happens; I only know a little bit of what has happened to me. I am sure you, also, have had some experience of it. It can happen in very ordinary situations, like feeling your hands in the dirt of a garden or lying on your back in a field. In part, it happens just through the physical touch of earth and sky and growing things. This physical, healing touch has to go deep within us to where we are truly broken. For me, the deep touching happens when my mind stops and my senses open and I am given willingness. I have never been able to do this for myself. It has to come through grace, in the Presence of the One I called the Power of the Slowing, the Wisdom of the Wild.

This Power, this Spirit, comes as It will and moves wherever It wants, in ways we can neither project nor control (John 3:8). It may call you to places very different from those I have spoken of, or come to you with another name. It may appear as She or He or It, or perhaps the Presence will drift like mists and emptiness beneath your senses and you won't notice a thing, except that you've become more open in the moment, more desirous, more here and now. And more freely, fully, naturally yourself.

Eleven
ANOTHER
WILDERNESS

Ah, who has the power to heal me?
Now wholly surrender yourself!
Do not send me any more messengers;
they cannot tell me what I must hear.

—SAINT JOHN OF THE CROSS, *SPIRITUAL CANTICLE*

Every time I returned to my daily life from those early trips to the mountain, I found myself pained by the loss of something dear. I desperately wanted to find a way to bring the Power of the Slowing home with me from the wilderness. I prayed to experience Her Presence and guidance in my busy civilized life as well as in wilderness solitude, but it did not happen.

No matter how hard I prayed or how diligently I tried to be open and welcoming at home and at work, She never showed up there. Old habits die hard, and I found myself trying to cope with the grief of this loss. I first tried to arrange my life so I could spend more time alone in the wilderness. I looked into buying some mountain land of my own, and even went so far as to place a bid on a piece of property close to the State Forest. I didn't feel completely right about buying wilderness, though. It seemed too manipulative, too controlling, and I found myself relieved when the deal finally fell through.

Then I got permission from the owners to camp in the precious place of fields and meadows where the giant matriarch tree lives, where I saw the little deer that was completely fear, where I found the turtle shell, and where I had so carefully measured the movements of the sun through the seasons. I built a lean-to and a fire pit there and spent many lovely hours at that place, but for some reason it never worked out for me to camp there overnight. I also went for more frequent day trips in my canoe; they were sweet and refreshing, but with all these attempts, I never again felt the Power of the Slowing come into me and guide me with the strength She had in the mountain forest.

By the summer of 1994, even the mountain itself felt different. I drove to Green Ridge in June and, to my shameful resentment, found that many other people had discovered its joys. Only a few years earlier almost no one had camped there in summertime, but now the place seemed crowded and I had to search for a site that promised even a little solitude. I finally found one, but on the second day a Boy Scout troop pulled in and set up camp a quarter of a mile down the hill. I was honestly happy that others were sharing this place, but I could not avoid a small proprietary anger: It was my place and I wanted to keep it for myself. And there too, even before the Scouts came, the Power of the Slowing failed to appear.

Intellectually, I understood—and I still understand today—that the Power of the Slowing will always be completely wild and free; She shows up when and where and how She chooses, according to the Divine Wisdom that She is. It was never my place to determine Her actions, only to respond to Her invitations. I also understood that in reality She is everywhere always, but that was no consolation, for I no longer could sense Her palpable Presence, the *feel* of Her guiding my steps. I missed Her terribly, but there was nothing I could do.

Very gradually, I began to notice something I had been previously unwilling to admit: I no longer heard the call of the wilderness. My yearning to be alone out there had disappeared. The Time of the Power of the Slowing had ended.

One day in February of 1995 it struck me that I should go to the forested mountain just once more, not alone but with Earl, my oldest son. I didn't question the feeling or make anything of it; I simply called and asked if he'd like to do it. The idea hit him as a godsend, something he really needed right then; the timing was perfect. So in the snowfall of a winter Friday we packed our gear and bought food for monster meals and went there, the first time I'd gone with anyone else, and it was indeed perfect. There were no miraculous visitations from a palpable Power of the Slowing—but by then I had given up hope for such manifestations and was "hoping" only for what would be. We sat for hours and watched the fire in snowflakes that the wind blew horizontally across the mountain. We were very happy.

By early spring I had finally admitted to myself that I no longer felt the call to solitude on my forested mountain. I still went frequently to sit and walk in the place of fields and meadows, and often on a weekend I spent the better part of a day in my canoe, but these were no longer seeking-searching-yearning times; they were simply times of seeing-feeling-experiencing what was there. There was much expectancy in me, but no expectations.

On one of those canoeing excursions I was healed of my addiction to fishing. It was the first really warm day of 1995, and I'd brought my fishing tackle and purchased a dozen fresh fat night crawlers. I put the canoe in at the boat launch near where the Franklin trees grow and paddled without a thought to a likely spot near the opposite shore where I dropped the anchor. Most people fish for crappie at that time of year, and they're there in abundance. I caught and released a couple of them, thrilled by the bites but somehow *sure* catfish also lurked nearby. Then I sat with my bait on the bottom, my mind wholly empty in the springtime sky and water, and I felt the rod move in my hand. It was neither a nibble nor a strike, just a movement. I watched the line where it entered the calm water and it moved, gliding steadily away from the shore, away from the canoe, away from me. I set the hook and the line went taut and the drag on my reel whined and the canoe itself moved with the pull, out and away until the anchor line reached its limit.

Concerned that the fish—and I knew it was a catfish—would break the line, I stretched my left hand out with the rod toward the fish and at the same time pulled on the anchor with my right. As soon as the anchor broke bottom, I felt the canoe move toward the fish. He was pulling the canoe, actually moving it, even while the anchor was still in the water. I got the anchor aboard by pulling the rope, grabbing it in my teeth, pulling again, and all the while the canoe was accelerating toward the middle of the reservoir, pulled by this calm, wonderful fish. He took me for a ride around the reservoir then, and other fishermen on the shore saw it happening and pointed. This time I took no particular pleasure in their attention; I was absorbed by the pure fun of being towed by this fish I had hooked.

The fish finally tired and I was able to bring him to the side of the canoe. He——or maybe she, as I saw the stomach bulging, perhaps with eggs——was huge, far too big for the little net I carry in the canoe. So I grabbed a piece of the loose anchor line and passed it through her gill-slit, up through her mouth, and tied her to the canoe. I immediately paddled back, the flames of fishing addiction burning high, to the place where I had caught her, and mindlessly put another worm on the hook and cast back into the same spot.

Almost immediately it happened again. Another huge catfish took the bait and took me for a ride, and again I secured it with a piece of anchor line. Back again to the same spot, only this time no bites. After half an hour, again without thinking about it, I paddled back to the boat launch. I got my camera and photographed the two fish and then released them without a single thought of broiling catfish steaks. I loaded up the canoe and drove home.

The next time I went out in the canoe I simply forgot to take fishing tackle. Somehow, in finally landing the big catfish of my dreams, my compulsion to catch fish was gone, and it has not returned to this day. Since I cannot walk very far these days, I have a little electric mobility scooter to help me get around. Last spring, I rode the scooter down a path to a lake not far from our house. I tossed a line in just to see what it was like. Immediately a nice bass took the hook, and—still sitting in the scooter—I reeled him in. He was really a beautiful specimen: close to four pounds, with exquisite coloration. As I released him, I realized that this had been the first fishing I'd done in well over a year. It was fun, but I felt no pull to put the line back into the water. Somehow, after those catfish towed my canoe in early 1995, I was delivered from an addiction that had had me irrevocably hooked. Now, with great gratitude, I can declare that I am free.

GREAT GRATITUDE

I've written a book about addiction, and people expect me to be an expert on the subject, but I'll never really understand how such deliverances happen. The healing of my fishing addiction is no exception. All I can say is thank you.

I didn't realize it at the beginning, but it was gratitude that was replacing my longing for the wilderness and for the touch of the Power of the Slowing. Gratitude was slowly filling my heart, and it was more than being thankful for freedom from an addiction. It was eventually to become the Great Gratitude: sheer, unspecified thanksgiving for absolutely everything.

At first I didn't identify it as gratitude; it felt like a growing sense of happiness within me. Sometime in the late spring of 1995, a friend casually asked me if I was happy. I wanted to respond with an absolute yes, but I held it back. Always before I would have equivocated. I would have said I was happy about some things and sad about others. Now I found myself wanting to say I was truly, completely happy. It felt very strange to me, even absurd. How could such complete happiness be authentic when there was so much suffering in the world—even when I'd just been to Bosnia where so many atrocities were being committed? Yet I felt I had to acknowledge the truth of how I was feeling. I said it aloud, as much to myself as to my friend: "Yes, I am happy. For the first time in my life, I can say I am completely happy."

It was a shock to hear myself say the words. For days afterward I reflected on the feeling, reexamining it, trying to find some fault in it. I wondered if it were another midlife phenomenon, finally and abysmally attributable to hormones. I wondered if I were going crazy. But always the feeling remained, a down-deep happiness and thanksgiving as steady and absolute as bedrock, without reason or excuse, completely without justification.

From day to day, week to week, happiness deepened within me. As I came to know it better and grew more accepting of it, I began to call it joy. The thought even came to me, *I feel so complete, so fulfilled, so grateful for everything; I wonder if perhaps I am going to die soon.*

During the first week in May I discovered a lump in my testicle. I went through a day of denial, and then a week of fear before I saw the urologist. Through it all, the gratitude never left me, nor did it even diminish. I completely gave up trying to understand, much less explain it. The gratitude remained, through the surgery of having the testicle removed, through the diagnosis of lymphoma, through the strange discovery of another kind of lymphoma in my bone marrow, through seemingly endless painful tests, and through the six months of chemotherapy that were to follow.

This was a new wilderness into which I was called, and the story of it is too long to recount here. I can say, though, that the joy and gratitude remained with me when, knowing that the chemotherapy would soon make me too weak to use my canoe, I sadly put her away in midsummer, long before she expected it, and through the countless times I sobbed to think how long it would be before she and I might again move together on emptiness and mists.

The joy and gratitude were also with me as, in my last week of physical strength, I closed down my lean-to, the one in which I had never slept, dug up the gear I had buried there, and cried and dug the hole even deeper and laid myself down in it with a pure desire to be in the earth, for her healing and out of sheer thanksgiving for all she had taught me about myself: what it means to be humble, humane, human, humus, humorous, earth herself.

The chemotherapy made me far too weak even to consider going back to the forested mountain, but I also found I had no special desire to return. That particular call was gone for me, but my youngest son, Greg, has been there, overnight and alone, in the very place where I first went.

Greg is a professional clown. Exhausted after a long tour with the circus, and wanting to be near the rest of the family as I went through my treatments, he returned home in midsummer. "I need some quiet," he said, "and I've been thinking about that place where you camp in the mountains. I've just been wondering about going there myself for a couple of days. I thought maybe you could tell me about it, you know, how to get there and stuff."

I can't communicate the joy I felt as I gave him directions to the site and shared my fatherly wisdom about what to take, nor the excitement I felt for him while he was there, nor my ecstasy when he returned, healed and dirty and smelling of fire-smoke, with peacefulness in his eyes. I made him tell me every detail of his experience. He said, among other things, that he had sat for hours by the fire, thinking of nothing.

The Power of the Slowing has never come to me again—at least not in the form in which I met Her on the mountain, and I don't expect Her ever again to appear like that. But there has continued to be a Divine Presence that has accompanied my journeys during the past ten years. Every living thing changes and grows, and as I have changed and grown so has this force of nature, this Power of the Slowing. It has no gender now, nor has it ever physically touched or moved me as She did. But it has taught and guided me in ways far too delicate to describe, many of which are so intimate they do not even filter through my ego and my will.

It has not all been pleasant, to be sure. I have suffered much, and my family and friends with me. First there was the chemotherapy, which nearly killed me twice. There was a time, during that particular treatment, when I lost touch with both the sense of gratitude and the sense of Presence. It happened at a time of full incapacitation, when I had the strength to do nothing but lie in bed and when it seemed I would stay that way for over a month. Then I felt neither joy nor gratitude, nor any guiding Presence. The only presence I felt then was my own, and a slight, glimmering Wisdom-knowing that presence *is* Presence; my own being is continually created within God's Being. It occurred to me then that maybe sometimes when we feel most alone and abandoned by the Divine, it is because that One is so very close to us that we can no longer make the distinction.

The sense of Presence returned soon enough, and I began a long journey of recovery—though I never felt really healthy again, not like I used to. I tried to chalk it up to getting older. But then, in the summer of 2002, I discovered I had congestive heart failure. A biopsy showed the cause: a form of cardiomyopathy so rare that it does not even have incidence figures in the United States. It's slightly more common in the tropics, and especially in children in Nigeria and Uganda. Why me? I don't have a clue. There is no known cause and no known treatment. All the cardiologists could do was manage my heart failure symptoms and evaluate me for a heart transplant.

I waited for a year and a half on the transplant list at Johns Hopkins. Then I began to collect fluid around my right lung, and a routine examination revealed that it contained lymphoma cells. So a transplant is no longer an option, and I'm beginning another round of chemotherapy. My heart is so weak that the same kind of treatment I had ten years ago would surely kill me. Still, they have found a milder approach that we hope will work.

Nor has the suffering only been related to my illnesses. Years ago our daughter fell into drug addiction and never really recovered. As is so often true with serious addictions, it is impossible to count how many times we got our hopes up for her, and how many times those hopes were dashed. She's in her thirties now, and we've had no word from her for over a year. I only got to walk in the woods alone with her once. I was, I thought, recovering from my first chemotherapy, and she was just out of a drug rehab center, doing her best at her own recovery. It was winter, and it was a delight for both of us to walk together in the snow. There wasn't any sense of the Power of the Slowing—I've realized I need to be alone for that—but I treasure the memory of walking with my daughter in the snow.

Betty and I often look at each other and shake our heads in amazement. What a roller coaster these past twenty years have been! I am overwhelmed when I think of the steady love with which she has gone through these years with me, and how our kids have loved us through their own pain, and how our friends have shared the depths with us, and how hundreds, perhaps thousands of people have prayed for us through these years.

Of course we've had our good times as well: tons of lovely laughter together, beautiful family times, gratitude and pride for our kids and grandkids. The little canoe went to Florida with Paul, as I could no longer handle it. He sent me pictures of his daughters, muffled in life preservers, paddling the canoe on warm Floridian waters. This past June, he also sent me a framed photo-

graph of his youngest daughter sitting by a campfire. Around the
photo he had written a poem:

AT PEACE

Barely dawn, the frogs and crickets wake me.
Cold in my sleeping bag.
I hold my tent flap back and see him,
Squatting next to the fire.

His old hat with a new feather.
Simple boots, rawhide laces.
His pipe smoke mixes with the campfire's,
Then carries the scent of bacon into my tent.

It's cold. I have to pee, but I watch him,
Just sitting there,
His arms across his knees, watching the fire.
The bacon sizzles. He is at peace.

Later, I feel his strong fingers around my waist
The rock ledge is inches from my toes.
Autumn-painted treetops blanket the world below us.
I'm afraid, but safe. Breathless.

Over moonlit sand dunes on Lake Superior,
He floats a Frisbee with perfect aim.

We play for hours past midnight.
The moon is bright, and we cannot stop laughing.

Late that night I hear his voice, strangely serious.
"Be very still," he says.
A skunk wanders past the front of our tents.
We are terrified, thrilled, silent.

I remember these things,
Because my little girl is curled up in my arms.
I smell the campfire smoke in her hair.
Her fingers sticky with marshmallows.

It is cold, and I hold her close to keep her warm.
The frogs and crickets will wake me first.
Maybe she will watch me watch the fire.
I will be at peace.

PAUL R. MAY
JUNE, 2004

When the Power of the Slowing first called me into the wild, I had a misty background feeling that I was being prepared for something. Those five years, from 1990 to 1995, healed a deep fracture in me and taught me how to live my own Nature. They changed me in ways I could not fathom at the time. Only in retrospect do I see that they were indeed a kind of prep school, getting me ready for an ever-deepening education in Nature, an ongoing trek through a wilderness that in truth has no end. As I said at the beginning, wilderness is not just a place, like the outdoors or one's own body or mind. It is also a way of being, being wilder, and as such it is endless. Wilderness is eternal.

And in truth, Wilderness is everywhere. You don't have to go tromping to the mountains or desert as I did. You may find it in a local park, an open field, or a small woods. As I have said, you may even find it in your own room, or in your own body and mind. All it takes is listening for Wisdom's call.

Regardless of how, where, or when you experience it, Wilderness changes you. You come out of it a deeper, wilder (more natural) *you.* I think, for example, of how Wilderness changed my attitude toward cancer. Before my times in outdoor solitude, I probably would have accepted the general cultural reaction to cancer and other life-threatening illnesses, which is to see them as enemies. During my first chemotherapy, I was struck by how many of my fellow patients spoke of "fighting" their cancers. Sometimes people referred to me as "battling cancer." I think it was wholly my experience of the Wild that made such warlike references feel wrong for me.

Instead, I had to include my cancer cells in the natural "is-ness" of things just as they are. The lymphoma cells are also just what they are—deformed perhaps, misguided for sure, wounded in ways that make them destructive, but in no way enemies.

Now when I think of my cancer cells, I recall the time in the snow when I looked where the pileated woodpecker looked, and saw the perfection of trees, each of which was in its own way deformed, scarred, misshapen, even rotting. So the deformed lymphocytes that wander through my body cannot be enemies. I do not hate them. Neither do I concoct some silly tree-hugging love for them. Like all other things in true Nature, they simply *are what they are.*

This has had implications for my attitude toward treatment as well. The civilized world around me, including the medical world, expects me to participate in strategies for management of my illness. Civilization looks for causes and explanations to form an *understanding* of the illness, which is the necessary first step toward devising an appropriate management strategy. It's very much like conducting warfare: understanding the enemy is a prerequisite for victorious strategies and tactics of battle.

I have no objection to such attitudes—when they work. And quite often, they do work. They achieve the desired results. But there are many situations, of which mine seems a good example, where one can exhaust every bit of one's intelligence, knowledge, and expertise, and understanding simply does not come. Things remain irrevocably incomprehensible, deeply mysterious. In such cases, one is confronted with a choice: keep on struggling for an impossible comprehension or relax and accept the essential mystery. I have never seen the first option lead to anything but rage and exhaustion. In the second option, contrary to popular opinion, there is the possibility not only of peacefulness but also of great hope.

During my first chemotherapy, I was often so sick that I felt I just could not go back for more. I could have turned that into a strategic decision, either forcing myself to show up for the next treatment or accepting defeat and preparing for death. But what I found myself doing in the face of the mystery and the pain was *simply to see what happened.* Like a wild animal, I formulated no plans for the next day. As Wendell Berry put it, "I come into the peace of wild things who do not tax their lives with forethought of grief."[16] Like a wild human being with my natural capacities for wonderment, I was filled with expectancy. Would I show up for the next treatment, or not? Most of the time, as it turned out, I showed up.

I'm aware that this looks and sounds way too passive for most modern civilized people. From the inside, though, it is anything but passive. It is alive, vibrant, dynamic, even exciting. Most of all, it is simply what Nature taught me about being who I am in this world, just as it is in this present moment, just as *it* is. I am a part of the whole situation. I do not have to perform an imaginary extraction of myself from things-as-they-are in order to respond accurately to them. This is why I say we can never begin to heal the damage we have done to the earth until our own souls find a way back to being who they are as part *of* the Nature we so care for. And that it is Nature Herself who must heal our wound and turn us toward wholeness.

So much for attempting to put it into words.

I have a sense now of the Creator of the Universe, full of exuberance, loving all things into being, bursting with cosmic delight in fashioning endlessly diverse and infinitely creative life. It is a splendor so vast that I chuckle at myself for any attempt to understand it.

And now I must laugh aloud, for I cannot help feeling I *do* understand something of it; I understand that all creation participates in creation. Created by and of the essence of an endlessly creative Creator, creation creates endlessly. No wonder we sometimes can't make distinctions!

Sometimes I can actually feel this creation taking place as a kind of play: love dancing in freedom. Love is the pervading passion of all things that draws diversity into oneness, that knows and pleads for union, that aches for goodness and beauty, that suffers loss and destruction. Love is the Power that births and grieves, the laughter that fills the heavens, the tears that water the earth. Love is the energy that fuels, fills, and embraces everything everywhere. And there is no end to it, ever.

Love dances in freedom, which is absolute spaciousness: the inner and outer and everywhere emptiness that provides limitless growing room for love's creating: infinite elbow room for love's play, complete openness for love's experimenting. Freedom is a playground with no fences, ever, anywhere.

Love creates, and it keeps on creating, and everything it creates also creates. And there is nothing but creation, for even what we call destruction is creation; all breakings-apart precede new comings-together that have never before existed and never will again.

We human beings are one of more than a million species of animals that share this little planet with more than another million species of plants, living by the light of a small star we call the sun, which is one of billions of stars in this galaxy, which is one of billions of galaxies in this universe, which is . . . God only knows. And it's all going on in overflowing splendor, lavish profusion, luxuriant exuberance.

What the Power of the Slowing taught me is what the Source of the All constantly yearns for: that each one of us will know without doubt that we are loved, and that we are intimately, irrevocably part of the endless creation of love, and that we will join, with full freedom and consciousness, the joyous creativity that is Nature, that is Wildness, that is Wilderness, that is Everything.

NOTES

1. Henry David Thoreau, *Walking* (New York: Houghton Mifflin, 1906), pt. 2, paragraph 35.

2. Others had said it before Franklin Roosevelt, including Montaigne, Bacon, and Wellington.

3. Years later, in the summer of 1994, I had the opportunity to visit Bosnia with a group of six other people. The first day there, waiting to pass a roadblock, I heard the voices of women and men talking. The sounds of their language were hauntingly familiar, but I could not understand a word. Later that evening, walking alone along a lakeshore under a full moon, I remembered. If I had a thousand lifetimes I could not explain it. I was sure it was the language of the voices in the stream.

4. Long after this experience, I did a little research on cicadas. If you happen never to have seen one, they are truly magnificent bugs, one to two inches long, bullet-shaped with beautiful eyes and lovely lace wings. The best-known species in North America are called "periodical cicadas" and carry what I consider the most appropriate scientific name of *magicicada*. Depending upon their specific "brood," they spend from thirteen to seventeen years as grubs underground, then emerge, mate, lay eggs, and die. There are also a number of other species, called "annual cicadas," that spend only a few years underground.

5. I apologize to cat lovers who like to think their pets are very contemplative. As independent animals, domestic cats are probably more contemplative than we human beings are most of the time, but domesticated animals, of any species, are nowhere near as contemplative as their wild cousins. Read Thoreau's classic second essay on "Walking," in which he poignantly compares the life of domesticated animals to that of their wild counterparts. His three essays on "Walking" are available, among other places, in a Houghton Mifflin edition from 1906. In paragraph 39 of the second essay, he speaks of his joy when "domestic animals reassert their native rights—any evidence that they have not wholly lost their original wild habits and vigor; as when my neighbor's cow breaks out of her pasture early in the Spring and boldly swims the river." His philosophical reflections of more than a century ago are verified by multiple neurological studies. Seminal work in this area includes: W. P. Tanner, Jr., and J. A. Swets, "A decision-making theory of visual detection," *Psychological Review* 61 (1954): 401–9, and V. B. Mountcastle, "The view from within: Pathways to the study of perception," *Johns Hopkins Medical Journal* 136 (1975): 109–31. Some recent examples (with references to earlier studies) include: J. S. Robinson, D. M. Murray, and T. J. Voneida, "The cat's response to stimulus difference as attention focus and cue," *Perception* 7 (1978): 437–47; S. Sasaki, K. Naito, and M. Oka, "Firing characteristics of neurones in the superior colliculus and the pontomedullary reticular formation during orienting in unrestrained cats," *Progress in Brain Research* 112 (1996): 99–116; and C. K. Peck, M. Schlag-Rey, and J. Schlag, "Visuo-oculomotor properties of cells in the superior colliculus of the alert cat," *Journal of Comparative Neurology* 194 (1980): 97–116.

6. In a late morning on a hillside above a lake in Bosnia I heard cicadas singing. The Bosnian cicadas sounded different from the ones I had heard in the

United States; their buzzing was higher pitched, raspier, harsher. As usual I first thought many bugs were singing, but as I moved toward them I realized there were only three, one in each of three small trees about ten feet apart. Again they seemed unresponsive to any sound I made, but each stopped singing when I actually approached its tree. Through sight or sound or something they sensed my presence and became silent when I came close. Like the cicadas on my North American mountain, I never saw them.

7. Thomas Kelly (1893–1941), in his now-classic *A Testament of Devotion*, describes our habitual images of time in much the same way. Instead of a stream, however, he portrays time as a ribbon that stretches from past into future, and by which we are bound. The bondage makes us "take time more seriously than eternity," he says, "and we are only freed by the in-breaking of Divine Presence." In glimpses of this freedom, we begin to see that "The Now is no mere nodal point between past and future. It is the seat and region of the Divine Presence itself" (New York: Harper & Row, 1941, 90–95).

8. I believe this was a mute swan, one of that large and especially beautiful species with the sleek curved neck. Mute swans were introduced to the Americas from Europe as ornamental birds for large estates. As such, they have been semidomesticated for countless generations. In 1966, not too far from where I live, a storm released a handful of privately owned mute swans, which became feral and began to breed in the wild. At this writing, there is considerable concern about the damage they are causing to other birds and animals. Often referred to as "bullies," they have been known to attack boats and overturn canoes, and there are substantiated reports of mute swans having killed dogs, young children, and aged adults. Perhaps it is not especially remarkable, then, that the swan I saw was so vicious. But I still wonder why.

9. A few days later, that same surgeon strapped on a sidearm and hopped a chopper inland to try to save the life of a Vietnamese child who had had a leg blown off. "Gotta try to help if I can," he told me. In the summer of 1994, I met a Croatian pediatrician in the devastated town of Gornje Vacuf in Bosnia. He was introduced as a hero who had repeatedly risked his life crossing the lines to attend to Muslim children. "The Muslims," he explained with a sad smile, "they have too many children, and they don't take care of them. They don't care so much about life." No one challenged him. He was supposed to be a hero. I stared at the broken tiles on the floor.

10. Naturalist-author Barry Holstun Lopez discusses such encounters between wolves and their prey as well as between native Arctic human beings and the animals they hunt. He calls these moments "conversations of death." *Of Wolves and Men* (New York: Scribner, 1978), 61–63 and 94ff.

11. In Ethiopia today there are women and men who live in the desert: wild, wonderful people who carry on the traditions of the desert monks of seventeen centuries ago. In those early times there were monks who spent years living on poles up high, and people would bring them food and drink, and they were called *stylites* because they spent their time up on those poles. In Ethiopia today some do much the same thing in trees. They live in the trees, and people bring them food and water, and they are called *dendrites*, from the old word meaning "branches." In 1997, for somewhat different but just as wild reasons, Julia Butterfly Hill climbed a giant redwood to keep it from being cut down. She lived in the tree for two years. She is now recognized as a modern Wild Wisdom Woman. *Legacy of Luna: The Story of a Tree, a Woman and the Struggle to Save the Redwoods* (San Francisco: HarperSanFrancisco, 2001).

12. Genesis 1:26–28 and 2:19.

13. And for the Alatamaha River (now called Altamaha) in Georgia, where it was discovered.

14. This story was previously published as "The Stag's Lesson," Shalem News, February 1993. Shalem Institute, 5430 Grosvenor Lane, Bethesda, MD 20814, www.shalem.org.

15. Rainer Maria Rilke, *Letters to a Young Poet*, trans. Herter Norton, M.D. (New York: Norton, 1964), letter 7, 1904, p. 53.

16. Wendell Berry, "The Peace of Wild Things," in *Openings* (New York: Farrar Strauss, 1968).